Calmdalas - Book2
Adult Coloring Book

Over 50 Relaxing Mandalas to Color
One image per page

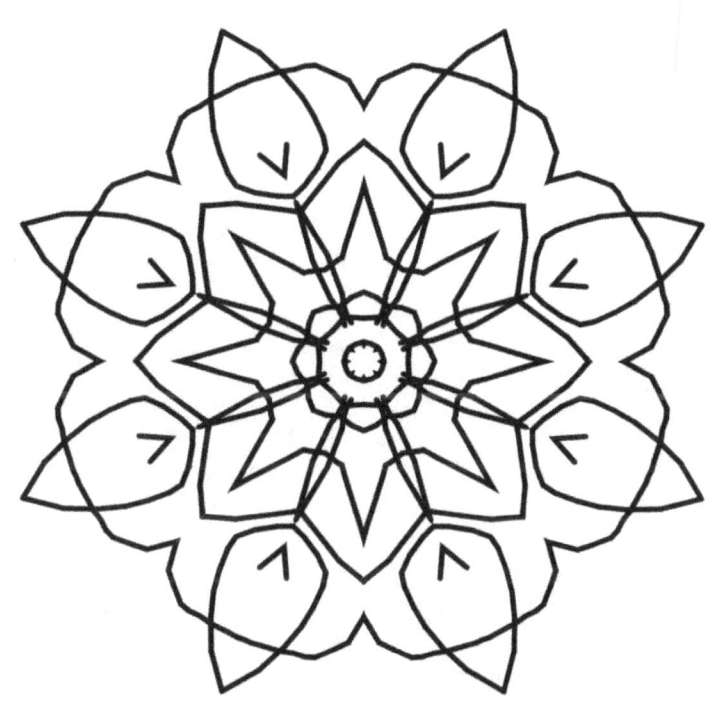

Sign up for our email list at www.calmdalas.com

Get notified about new books and get 10 **FREE** Calmdalas!

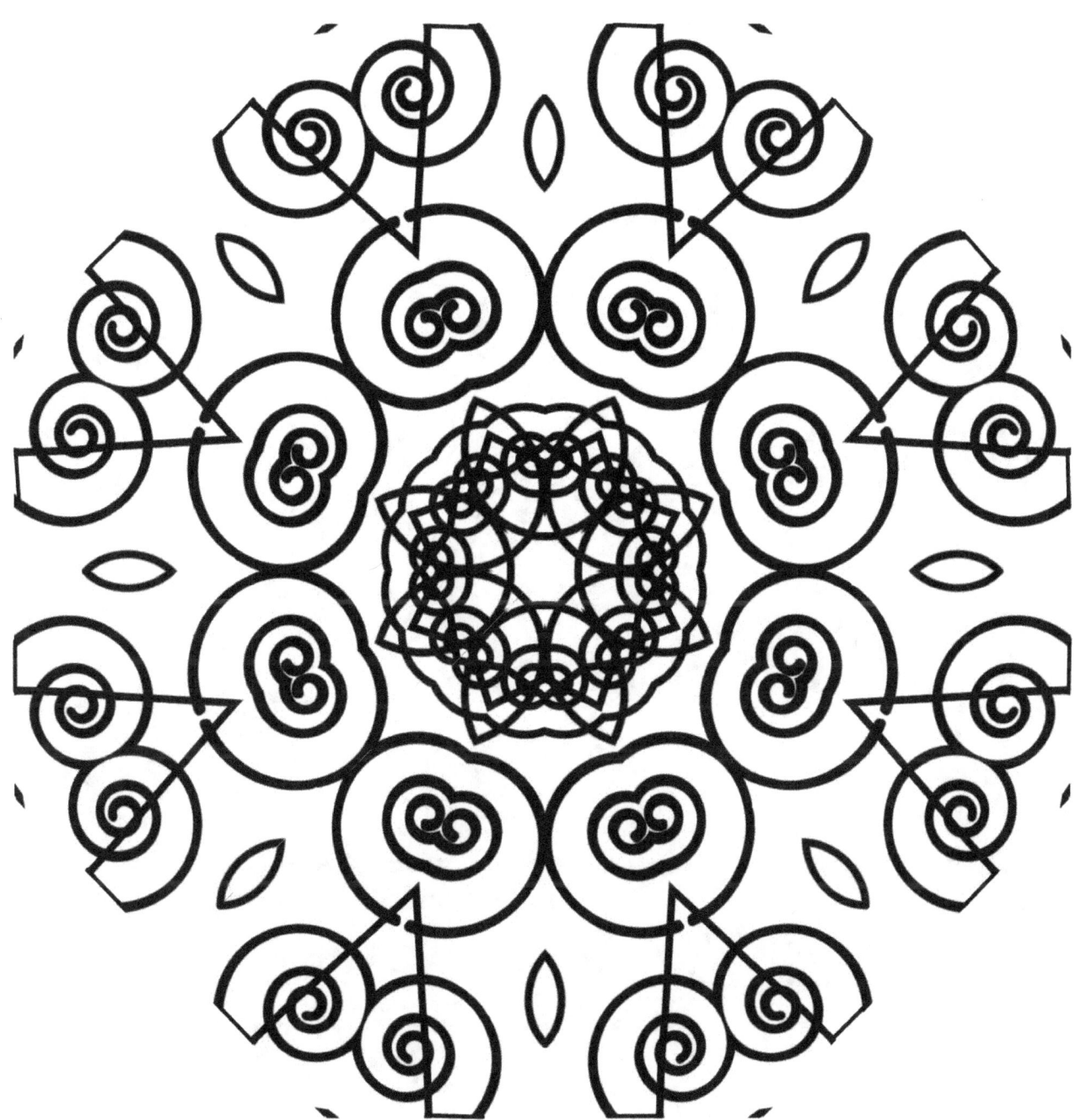

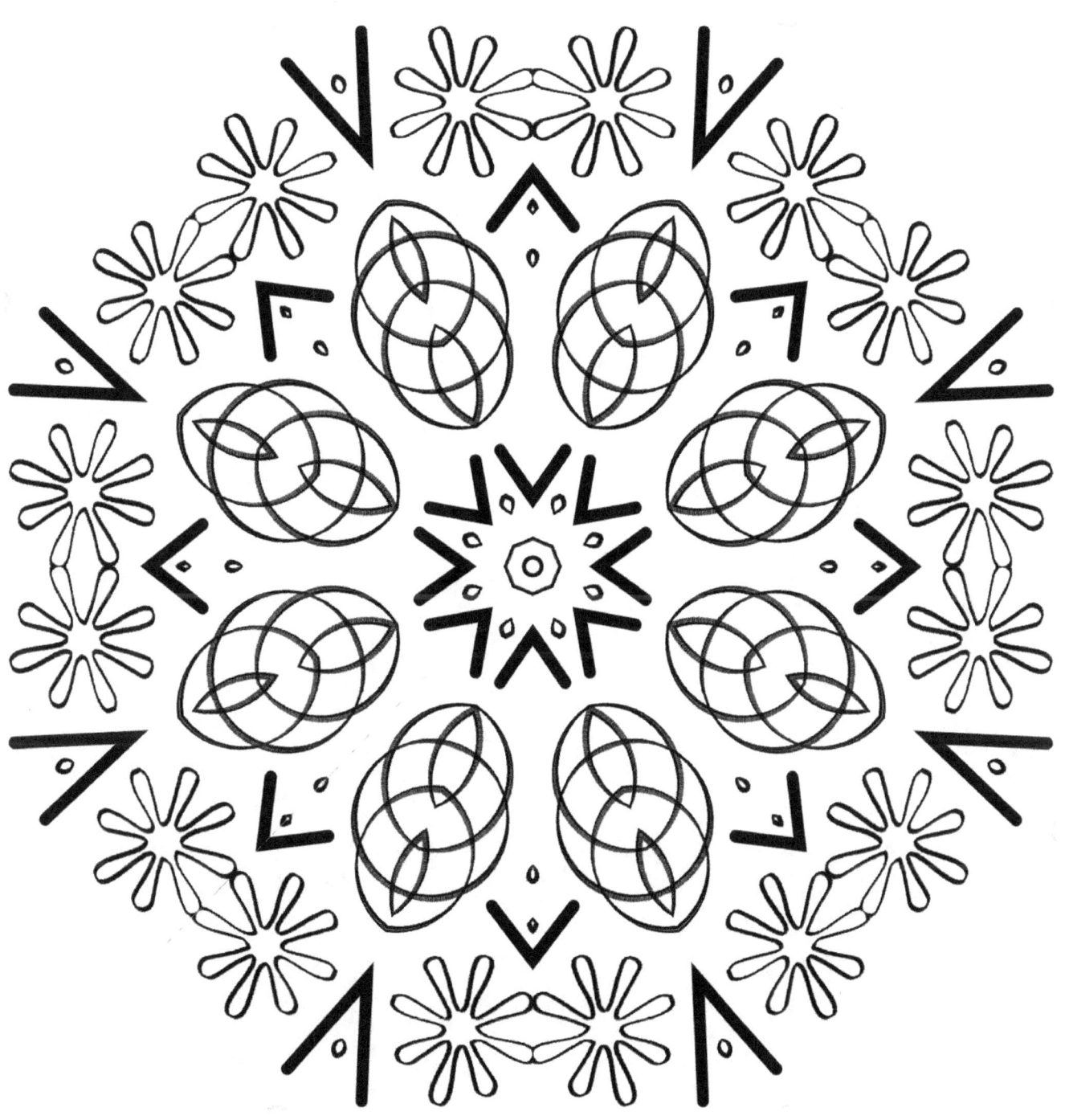

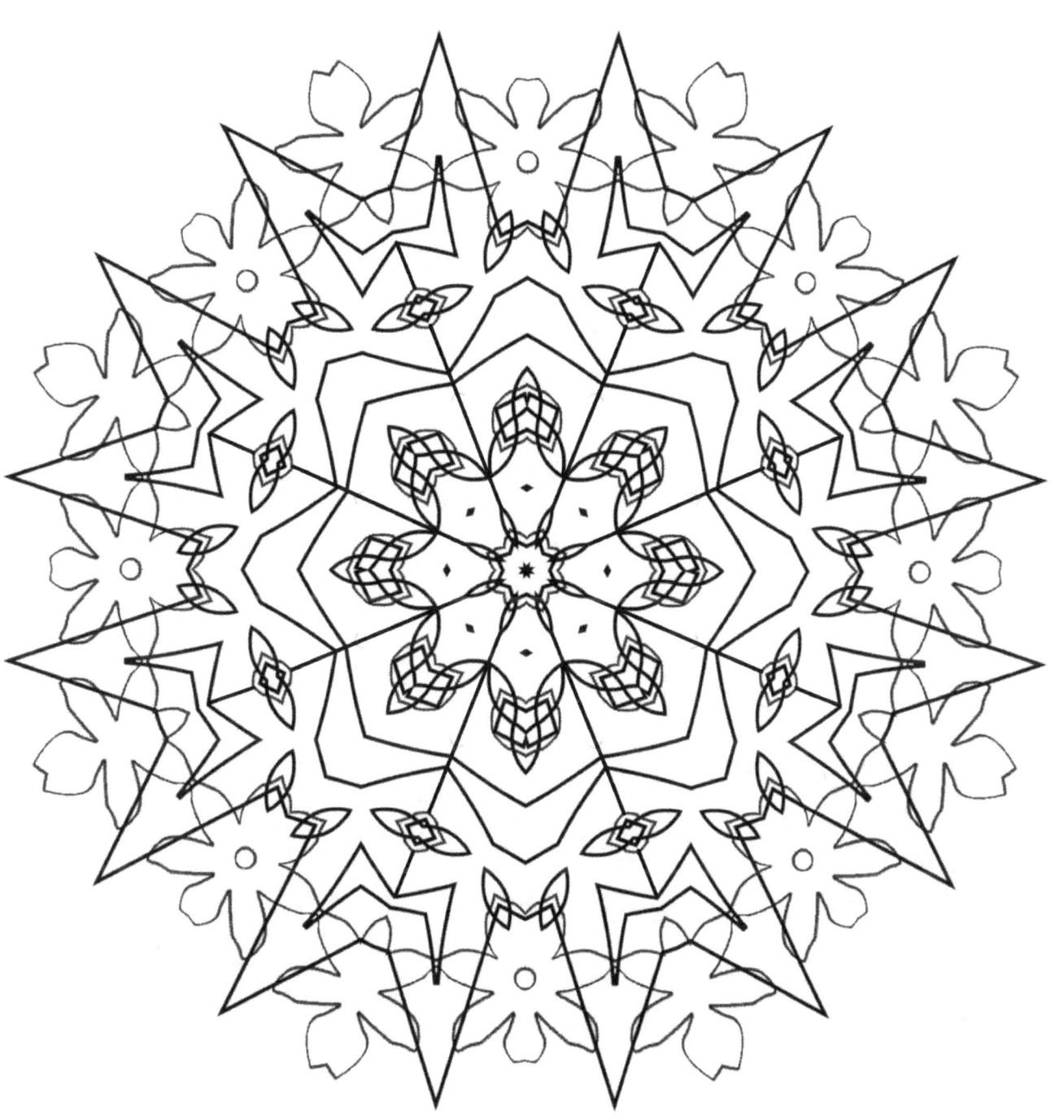

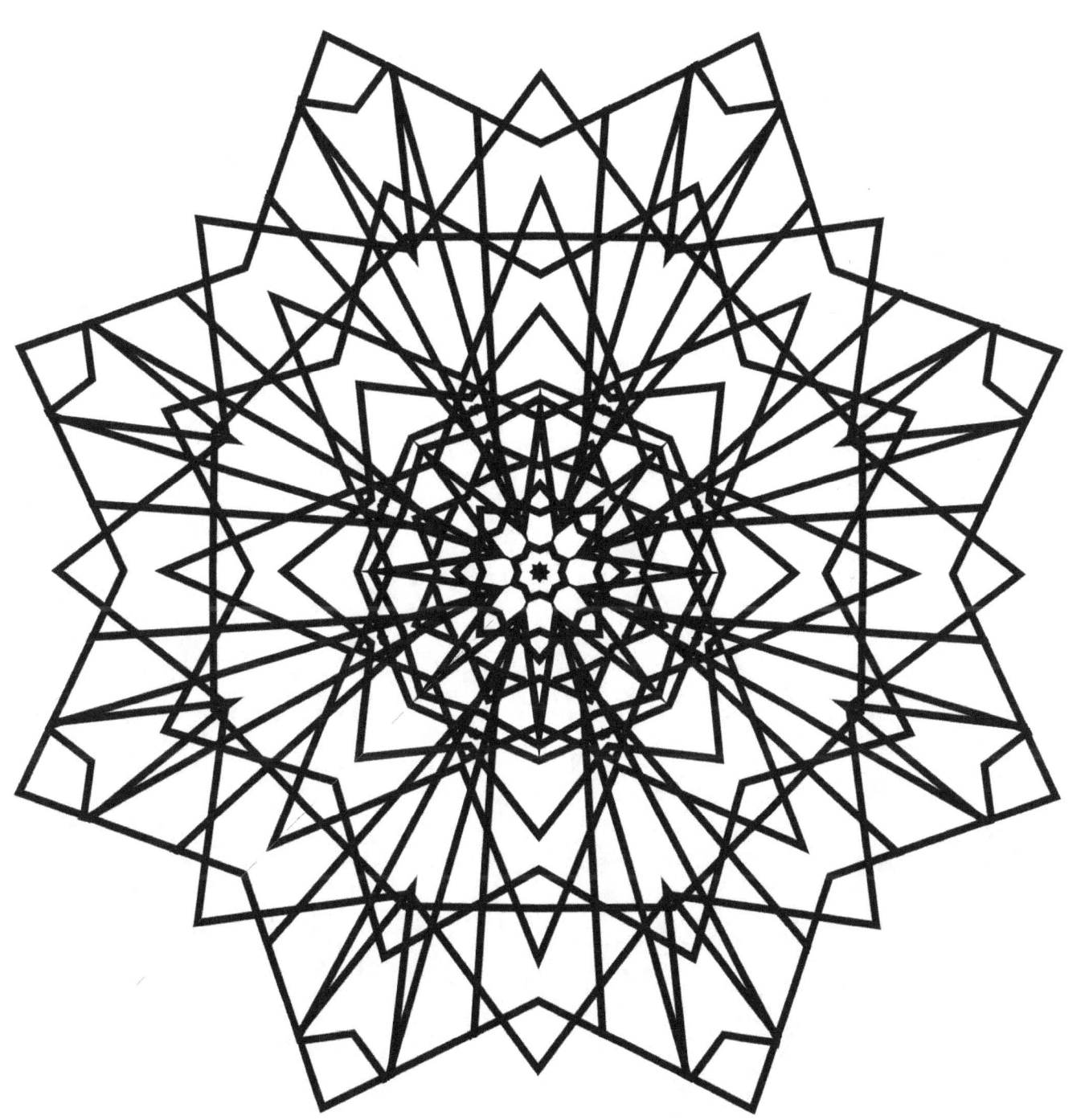

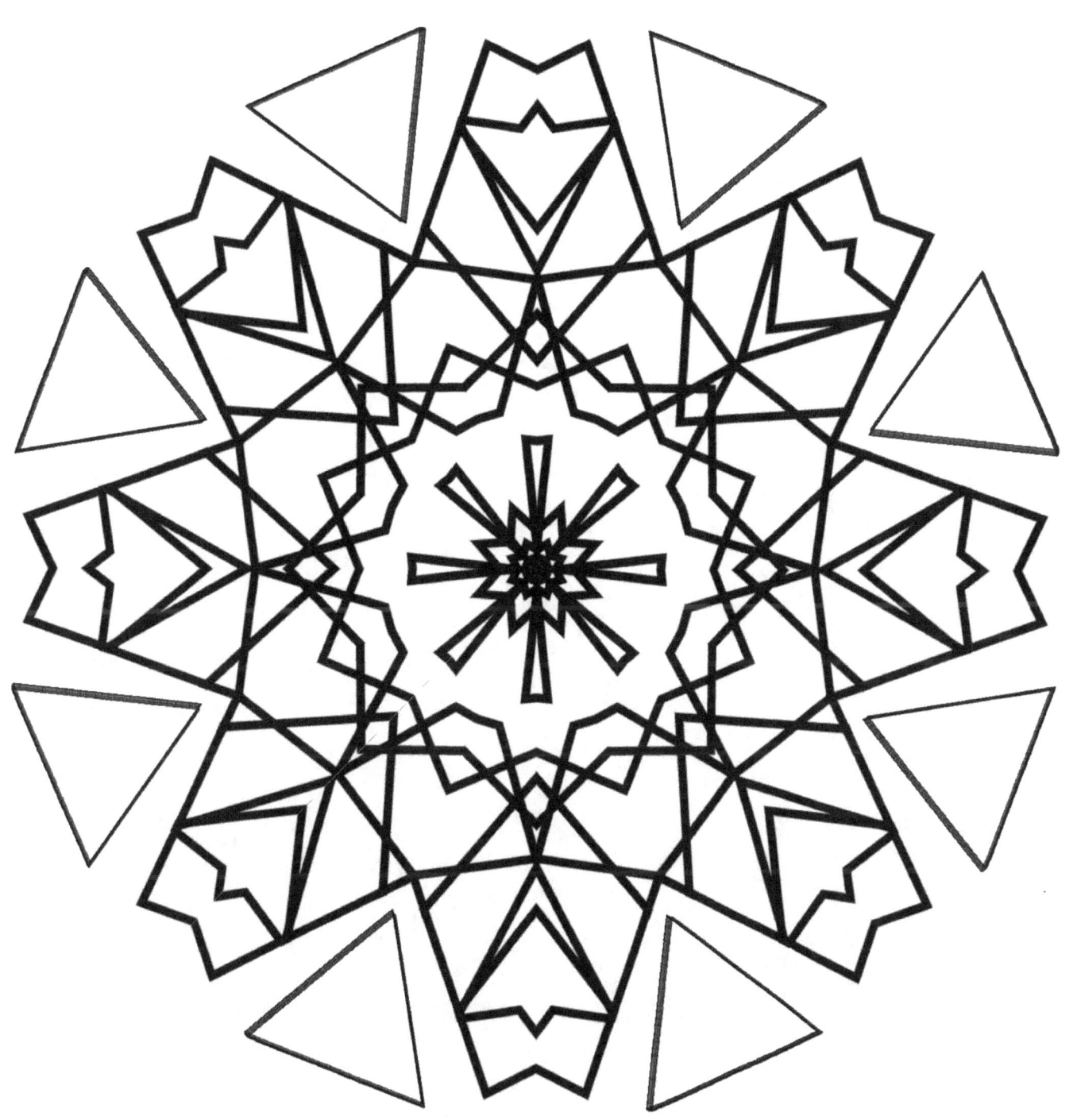

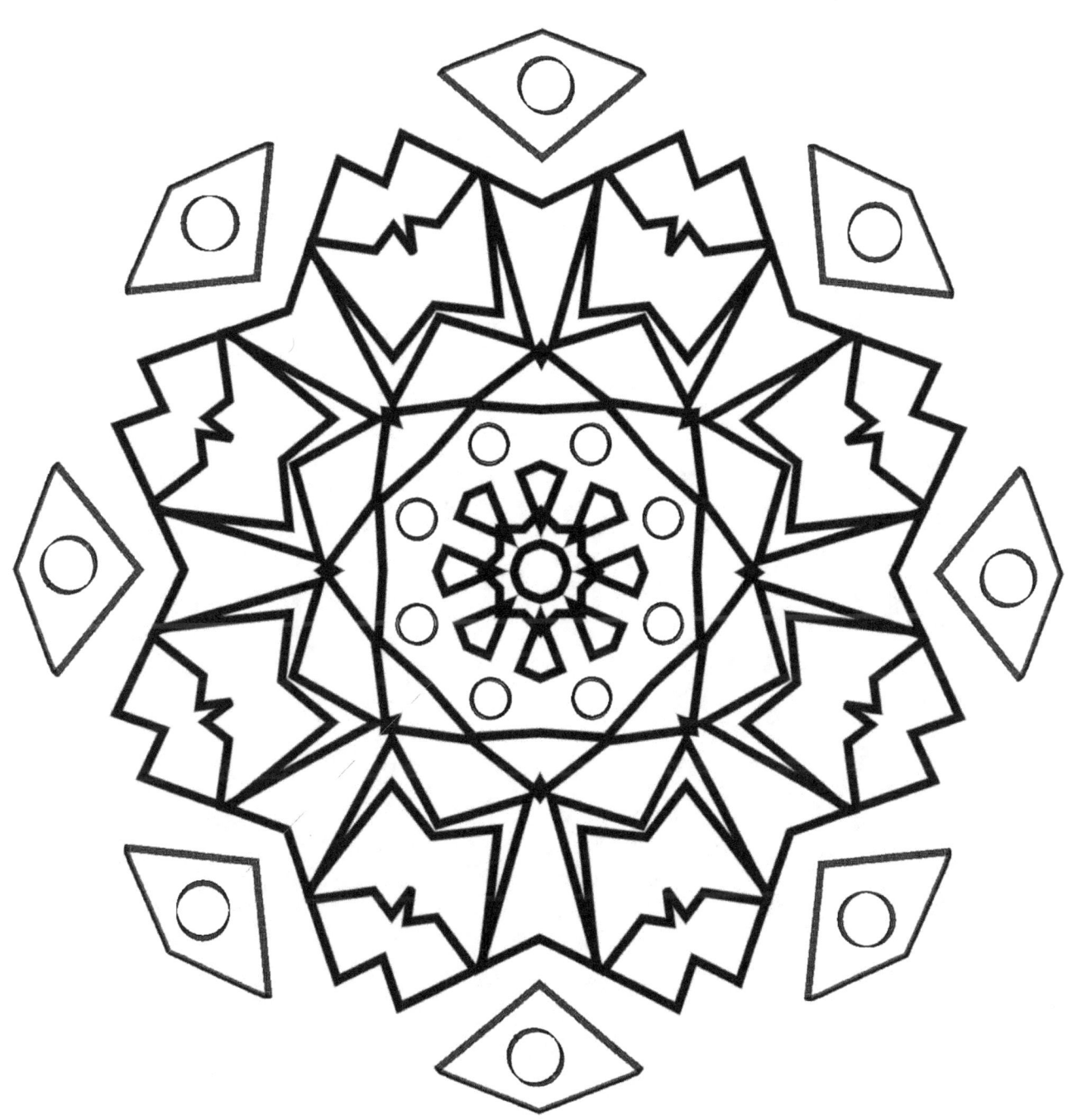

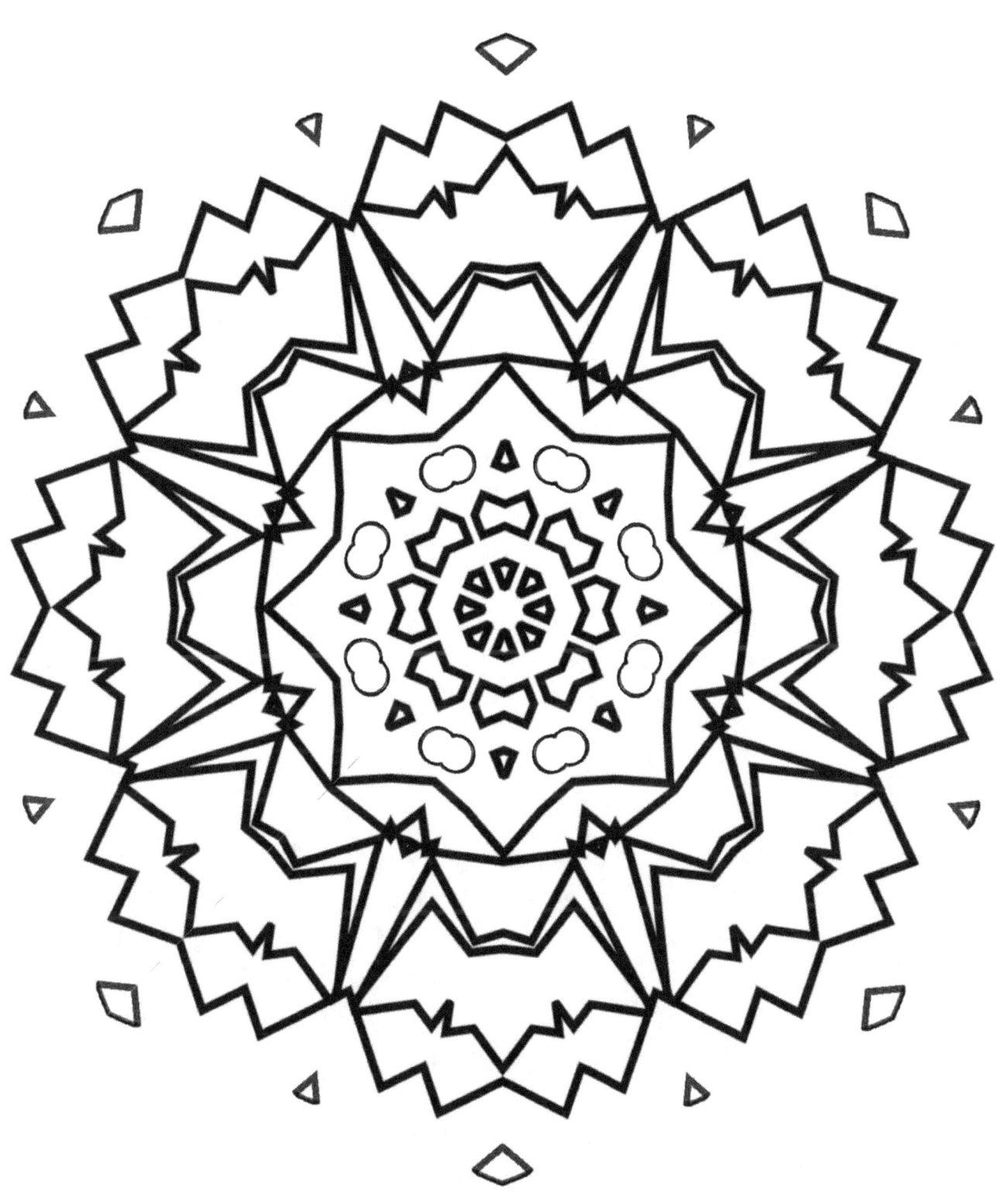

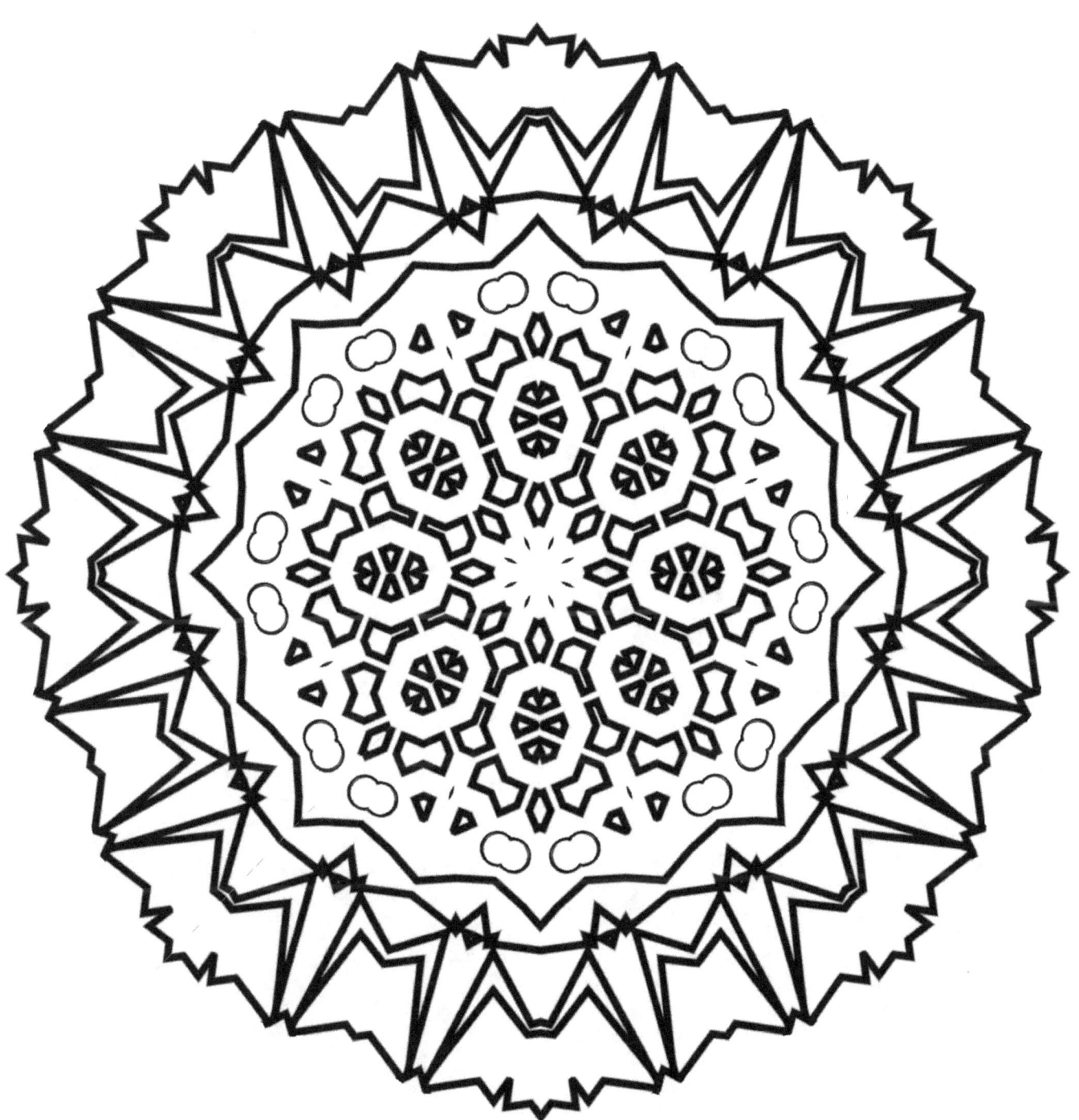

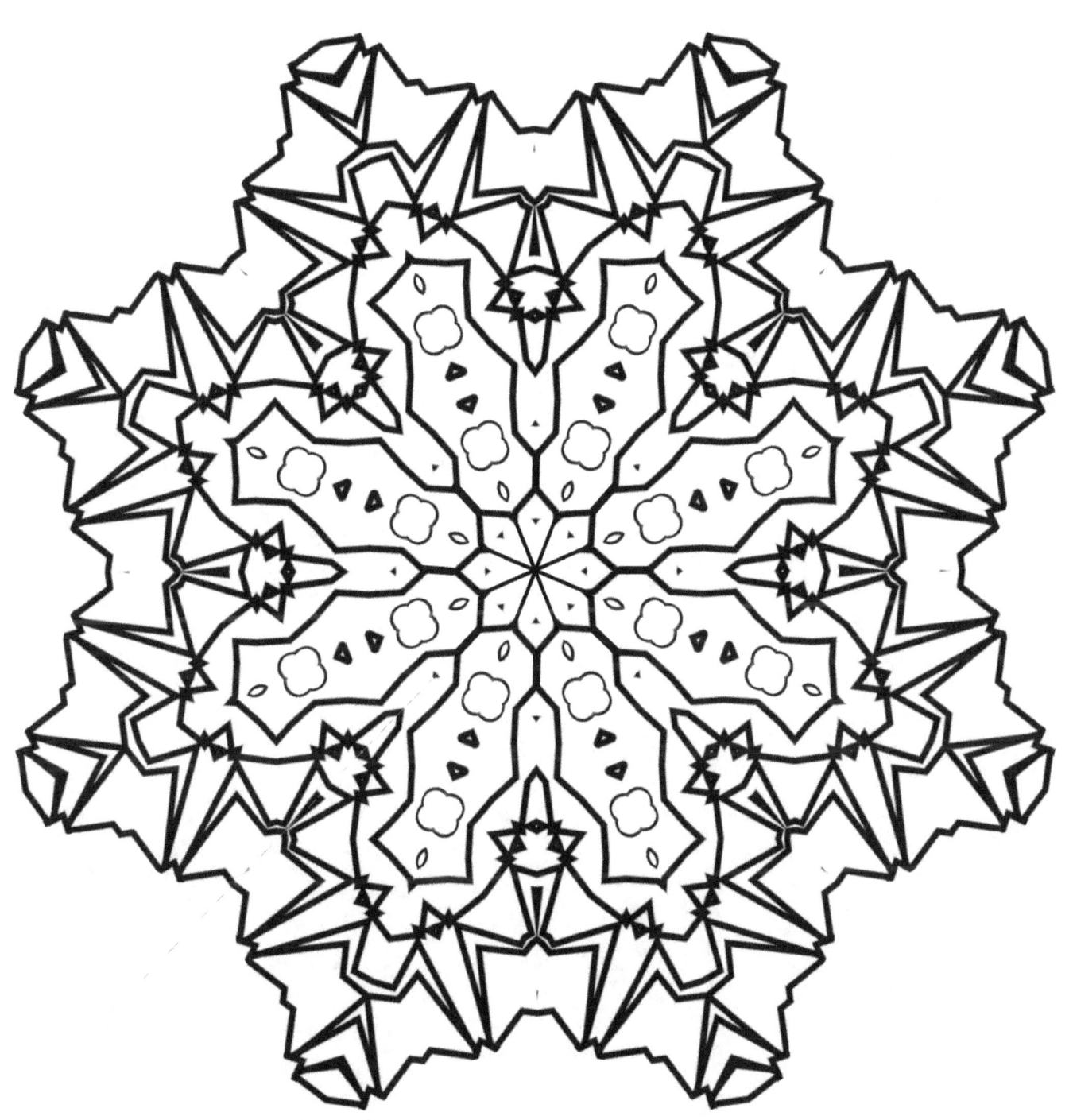

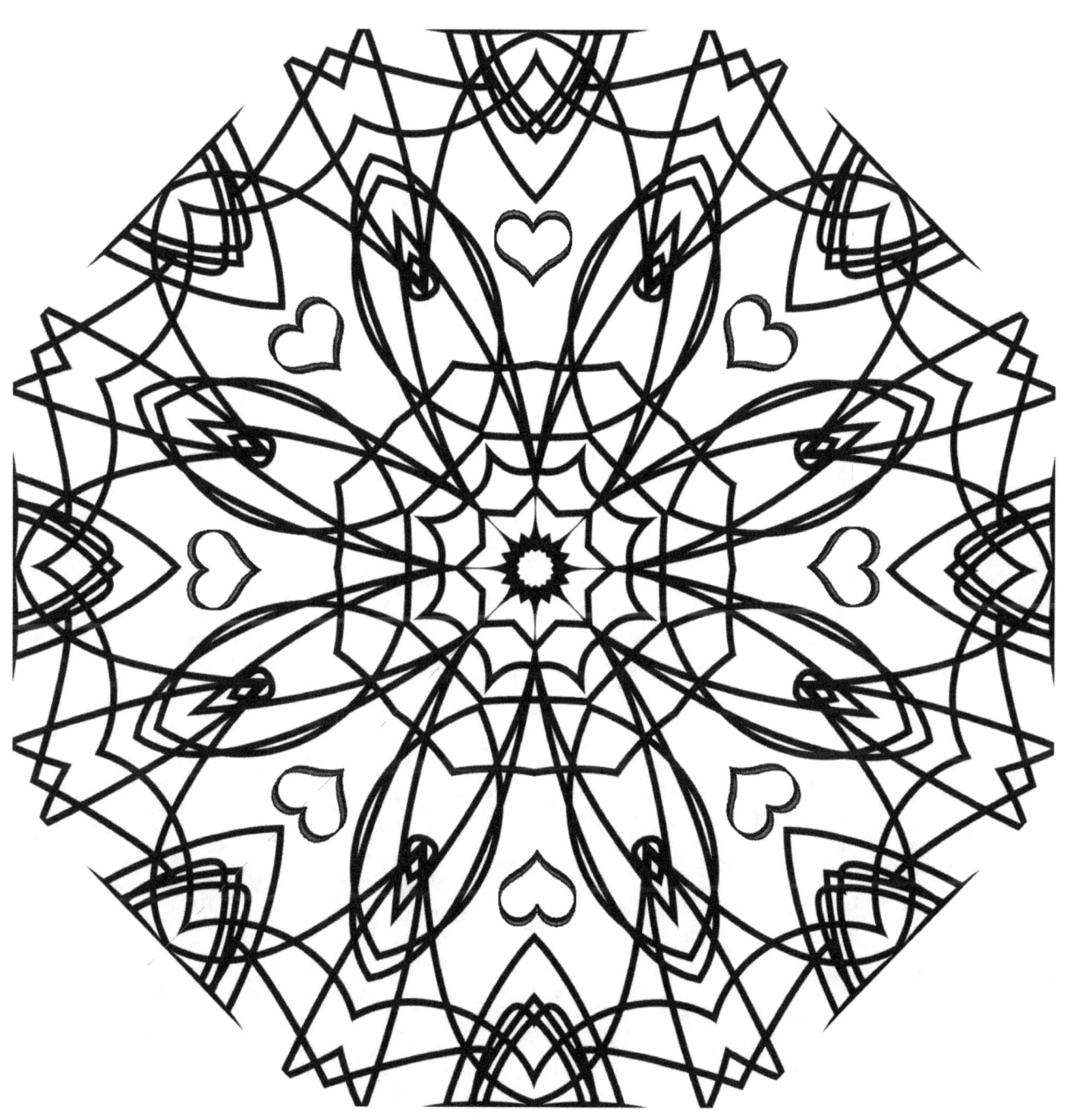

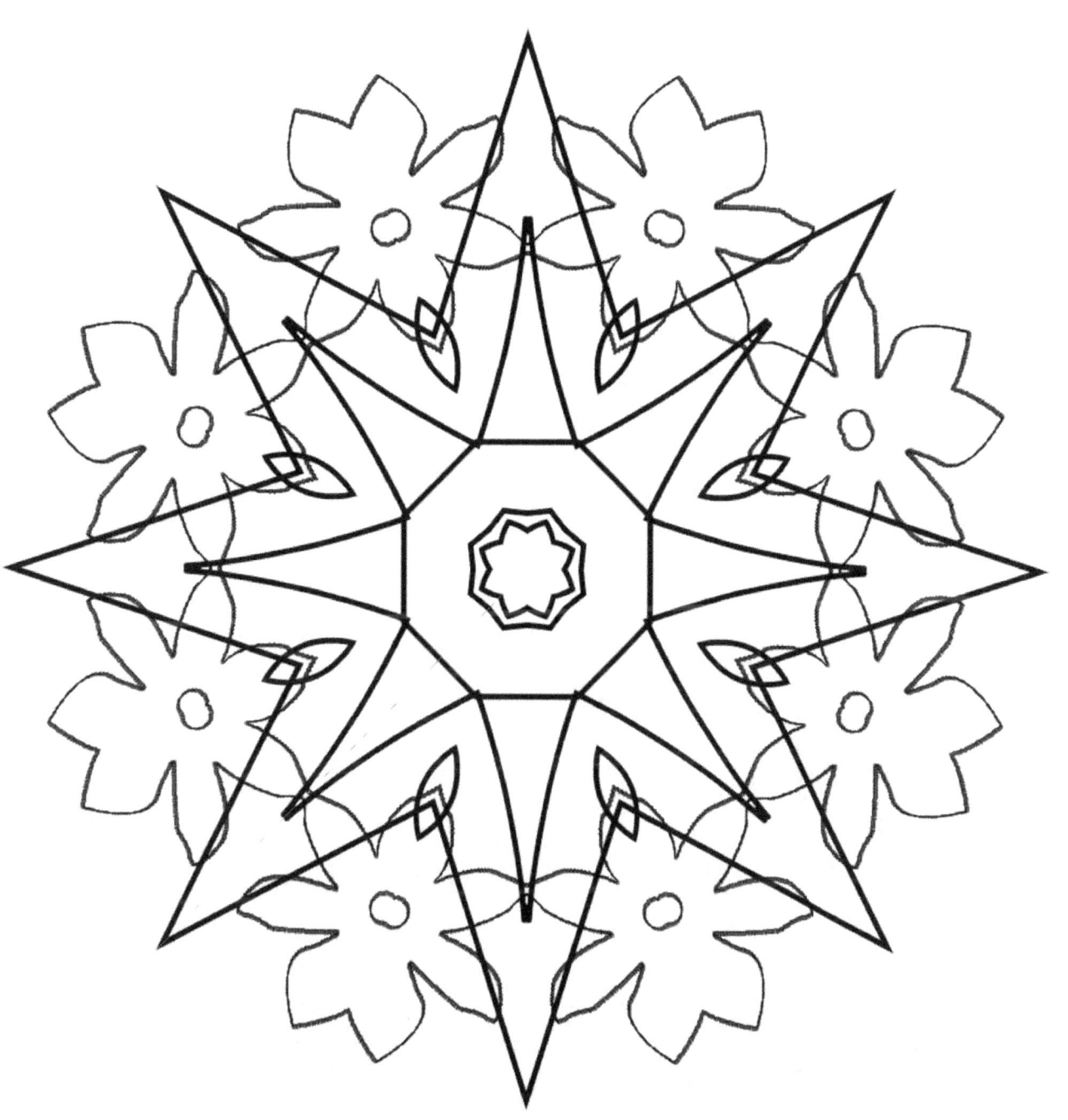

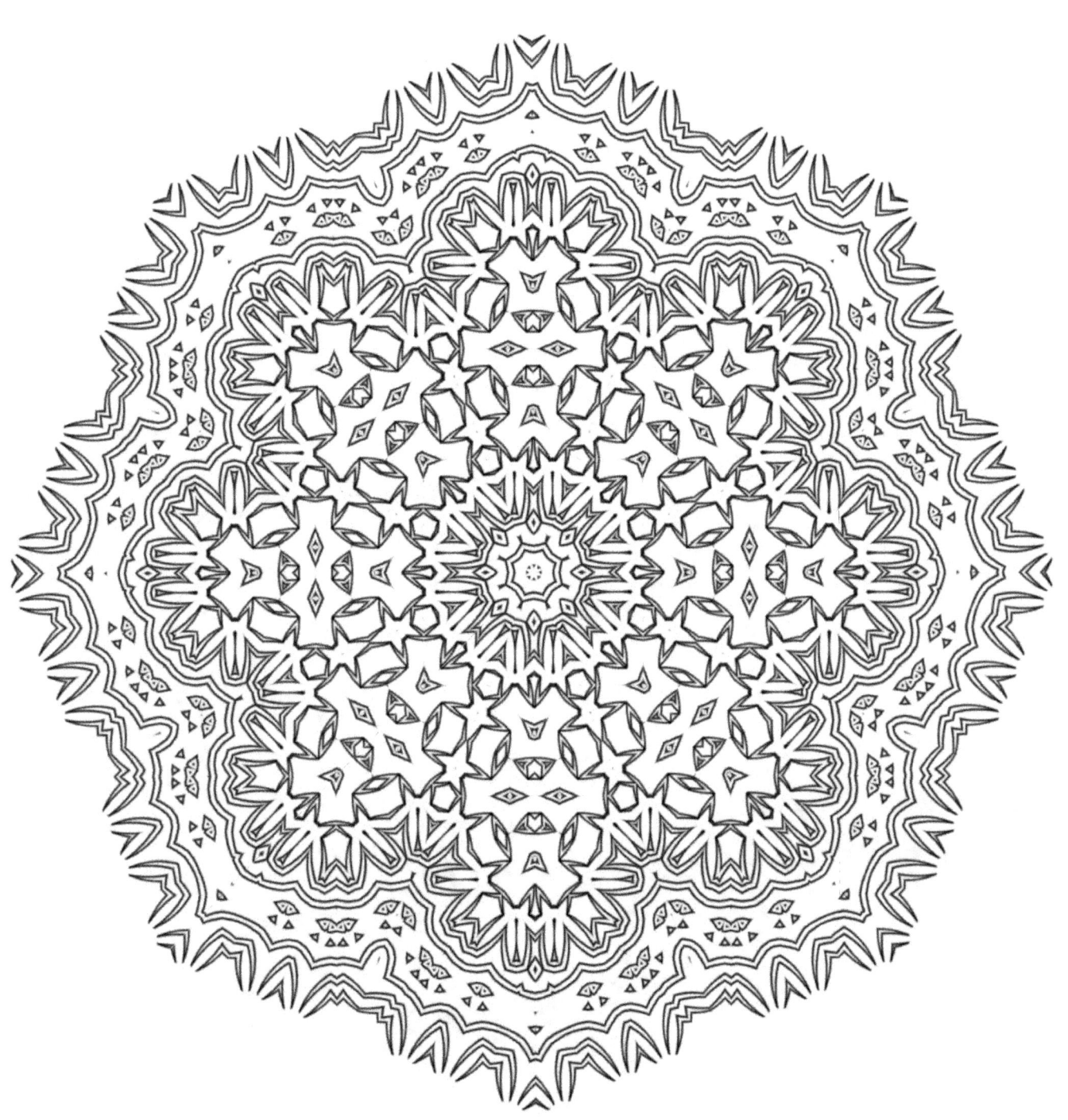

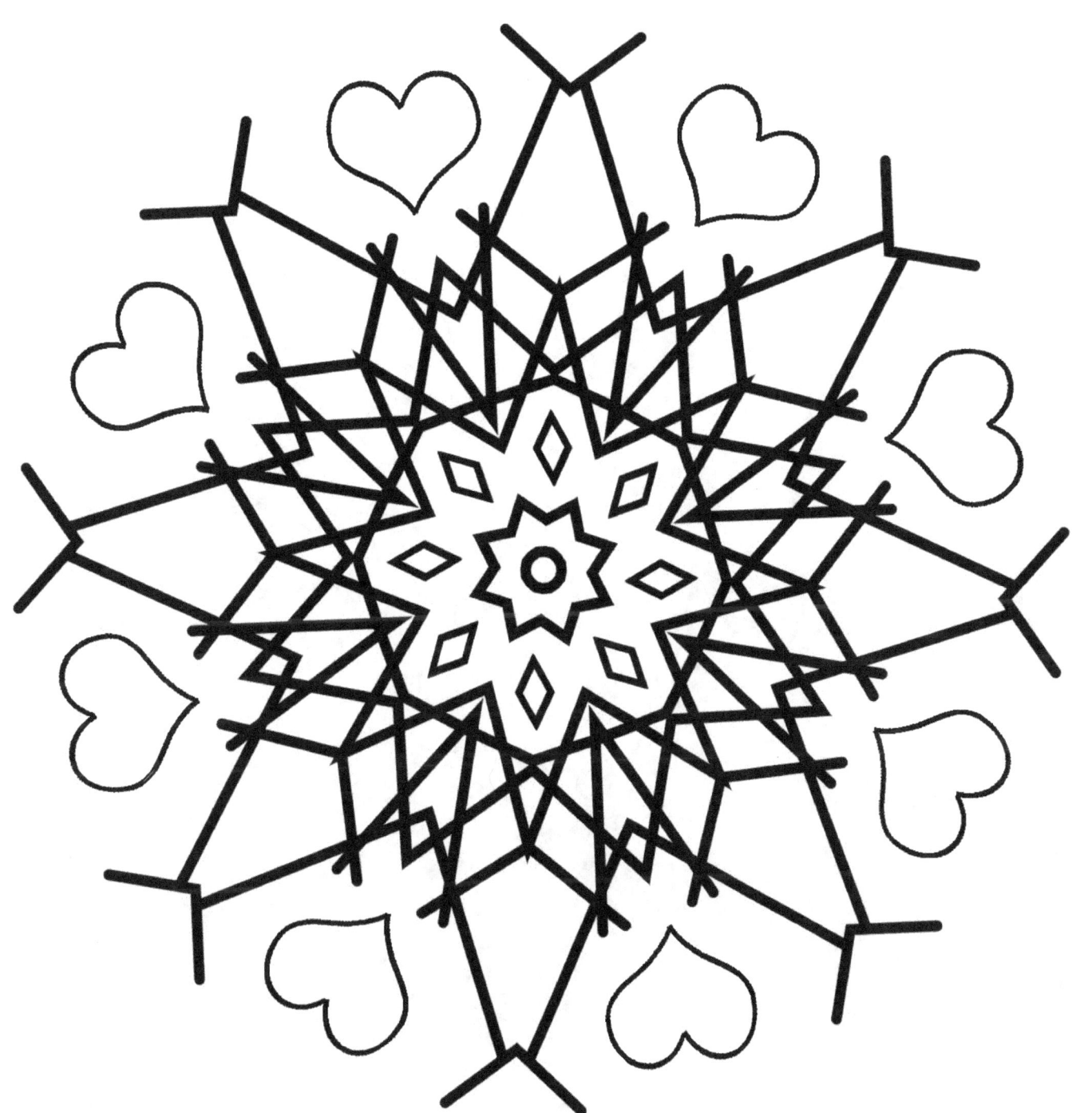

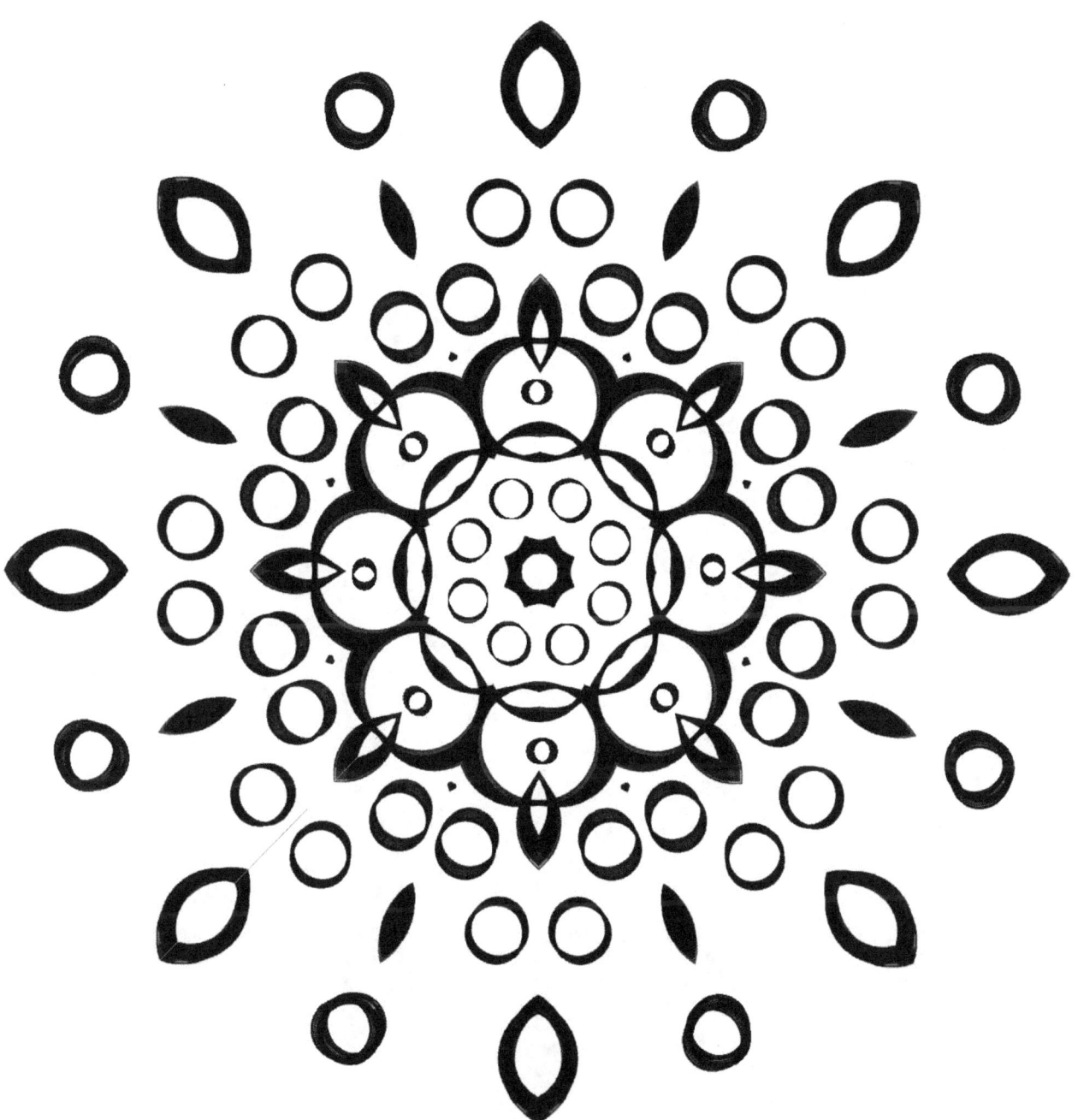

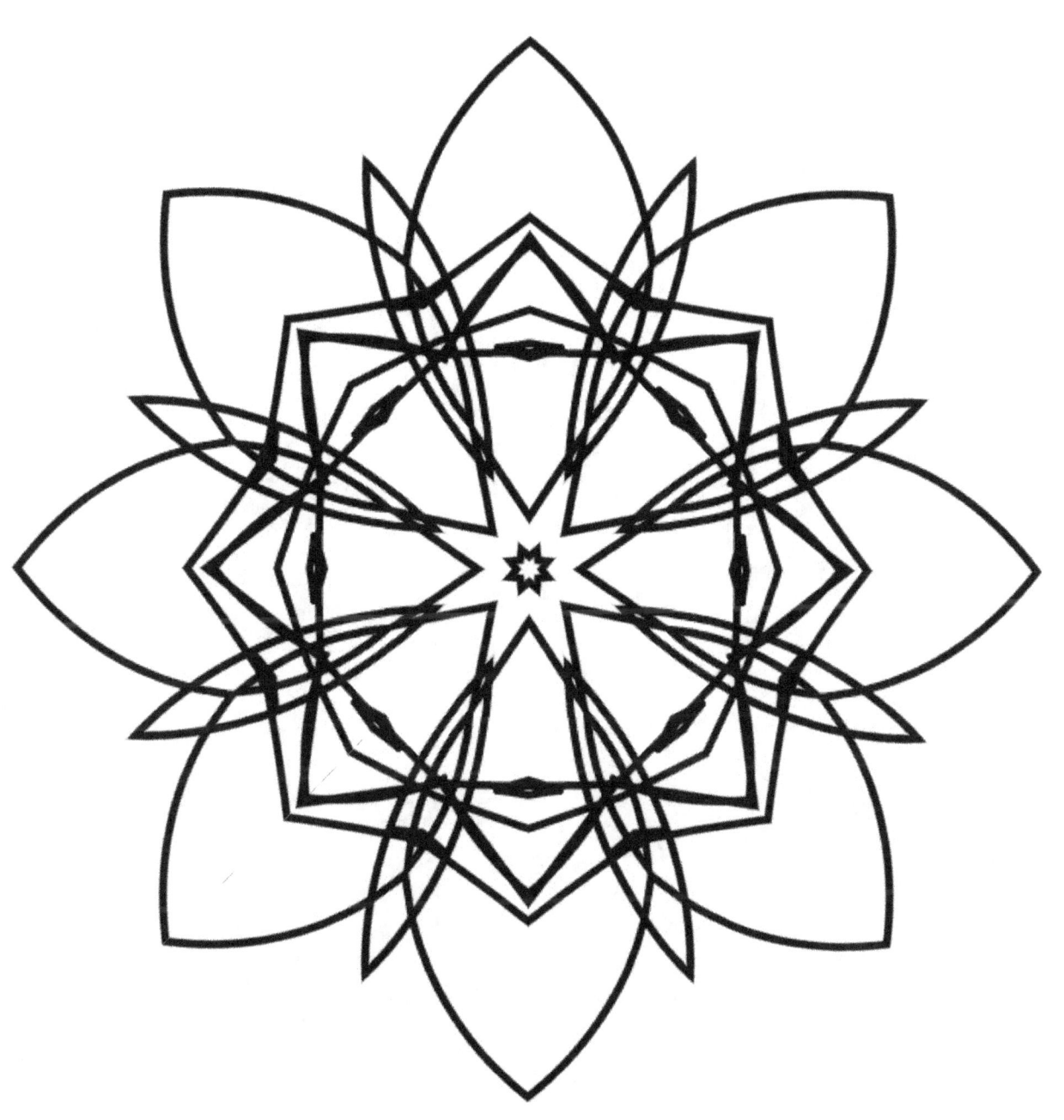

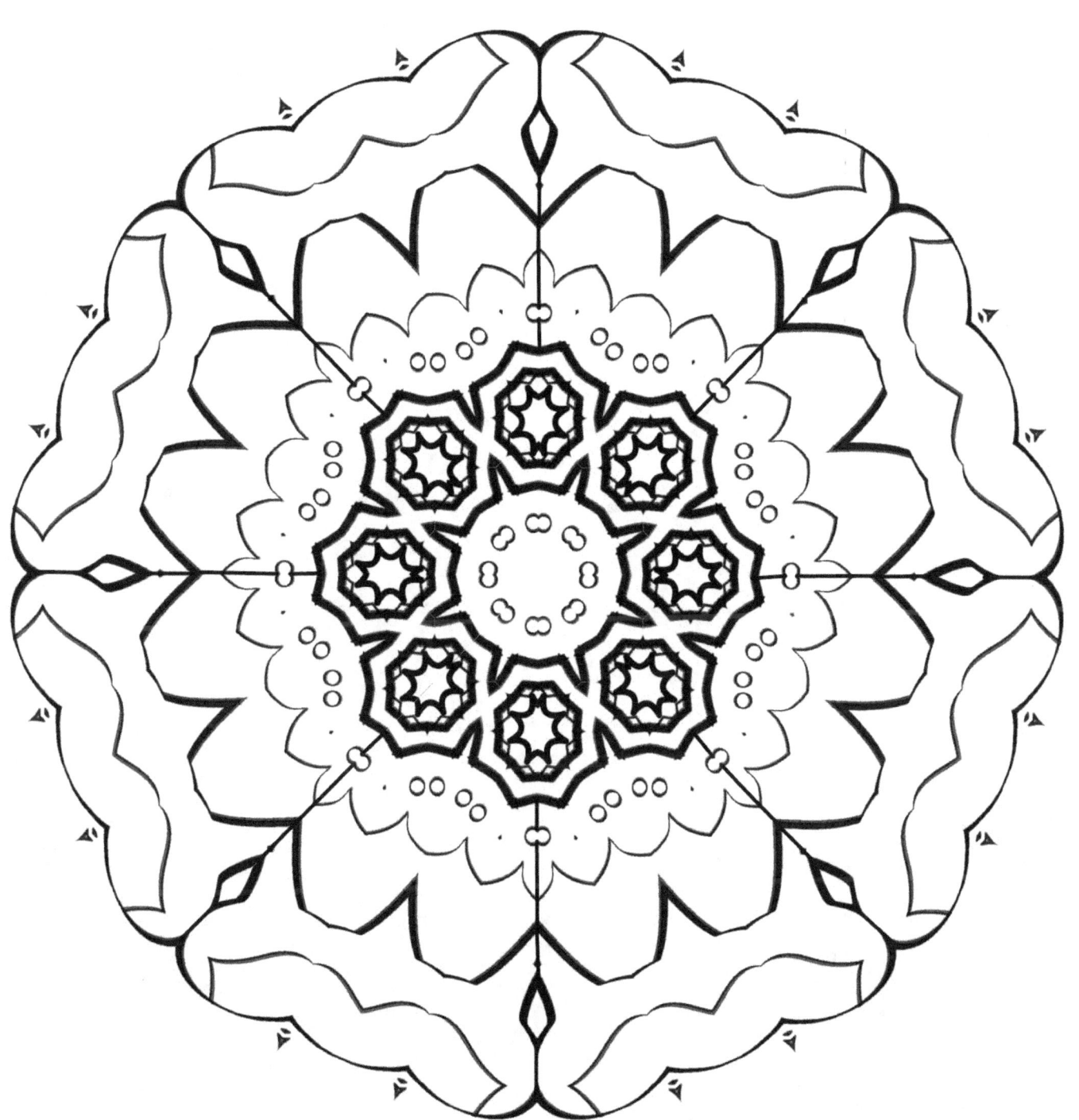

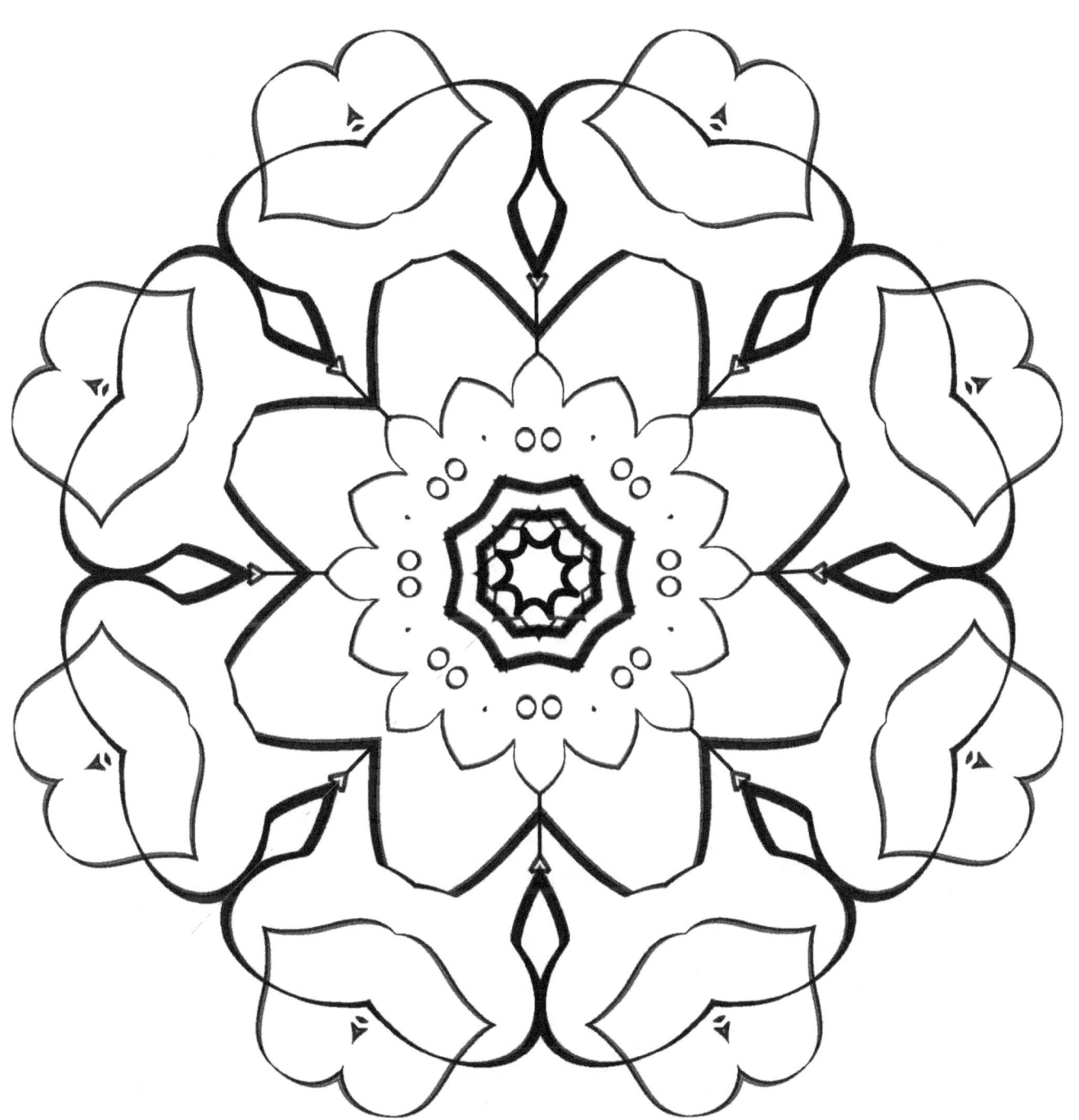

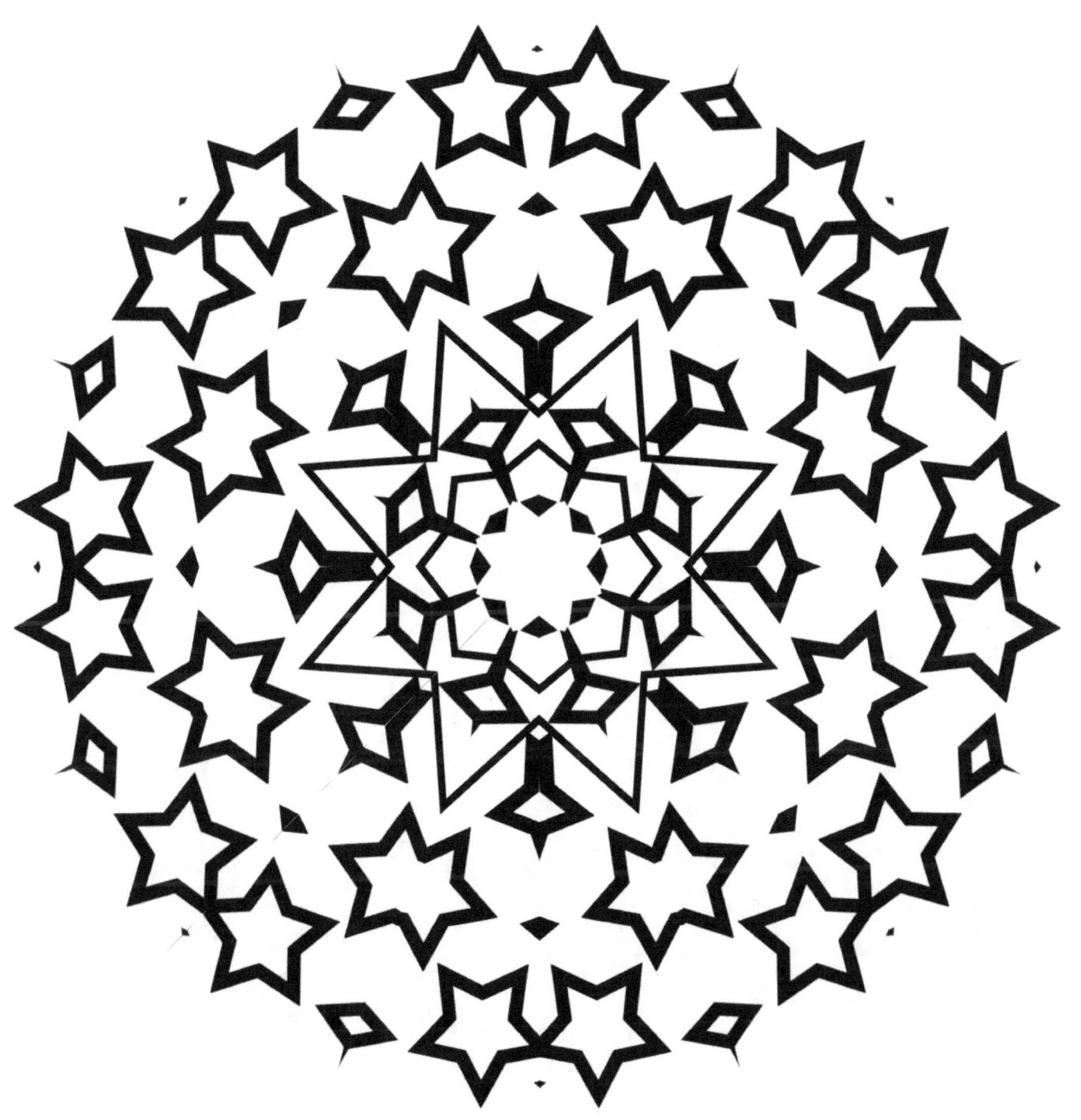

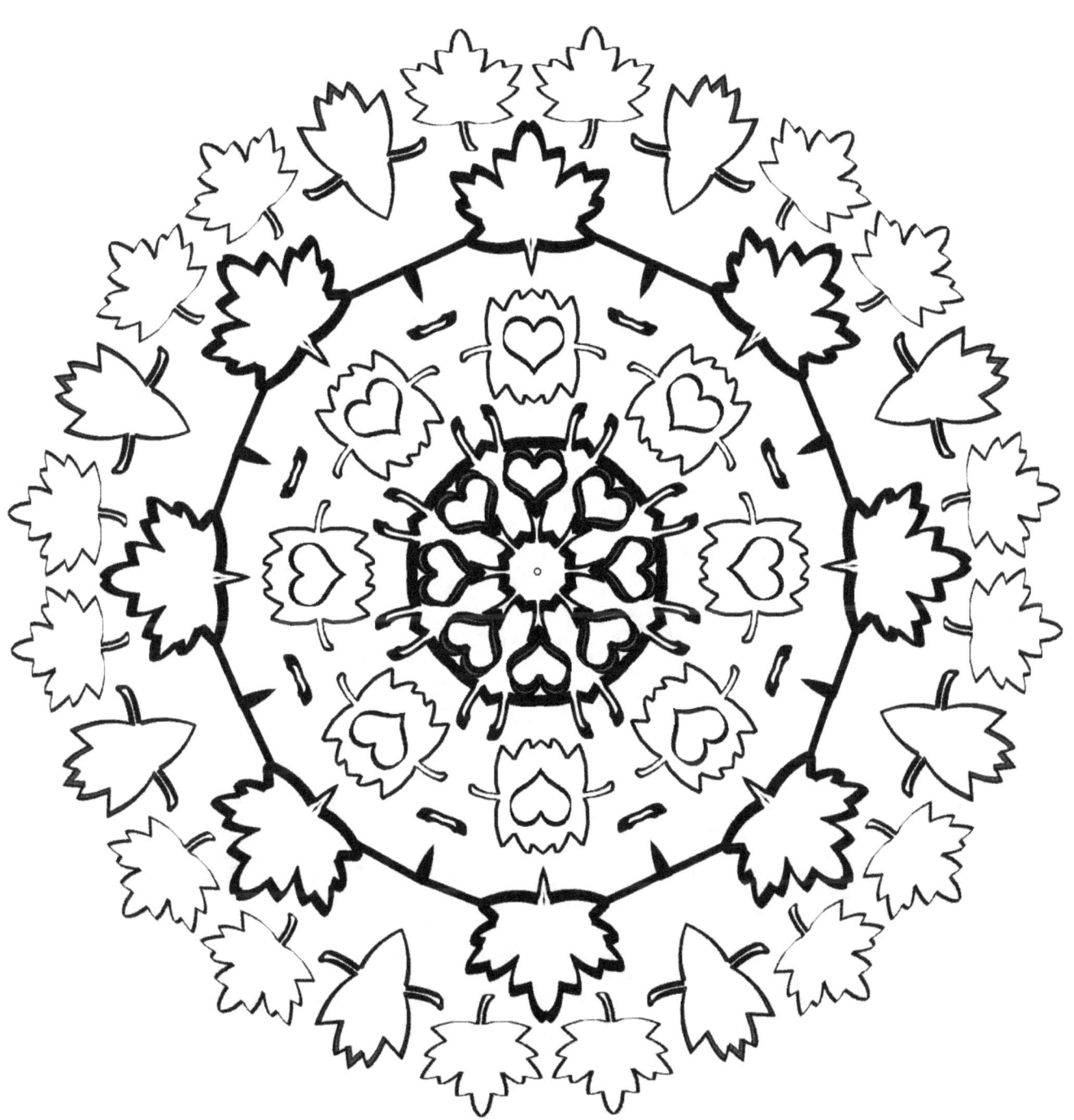

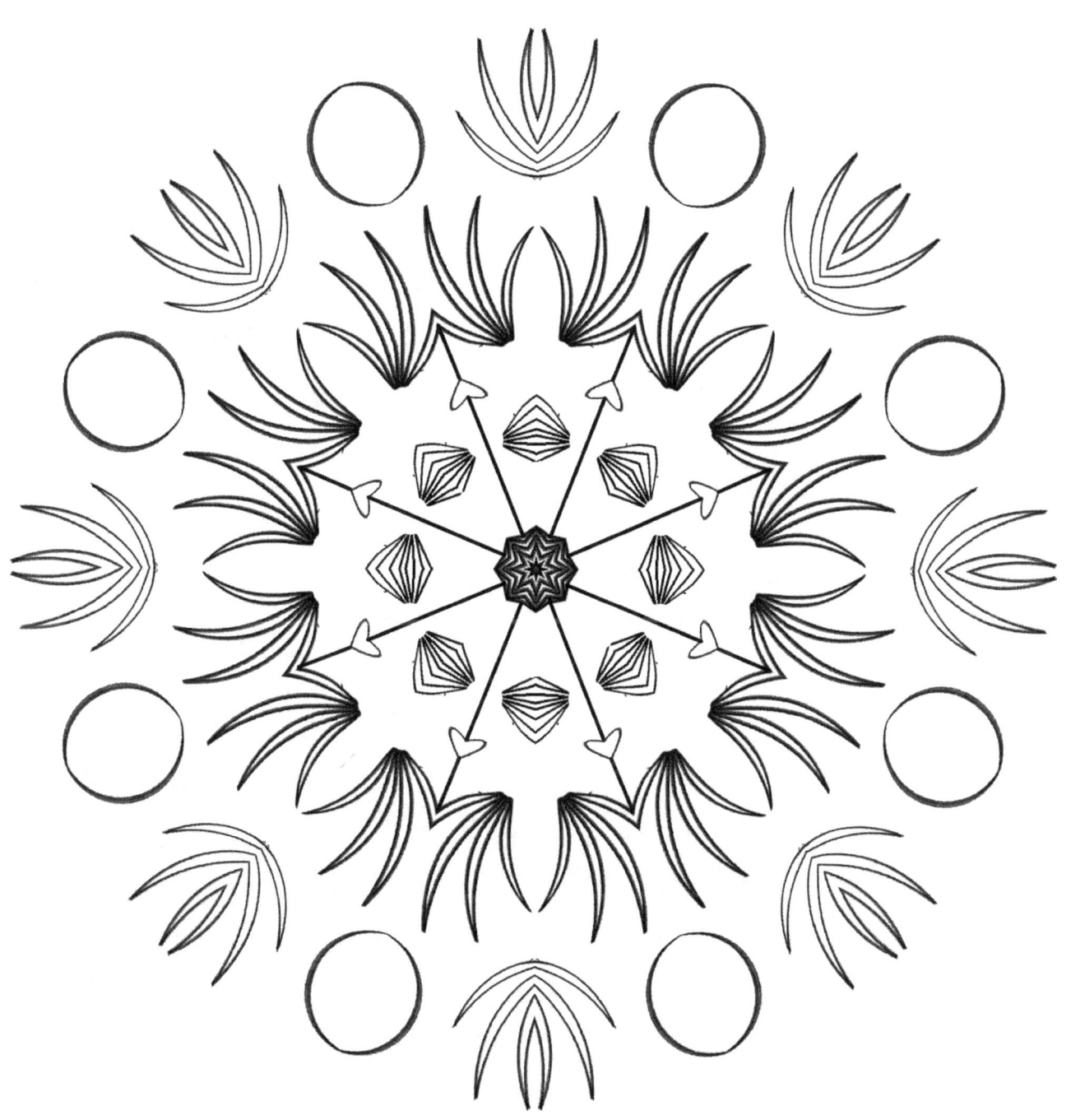

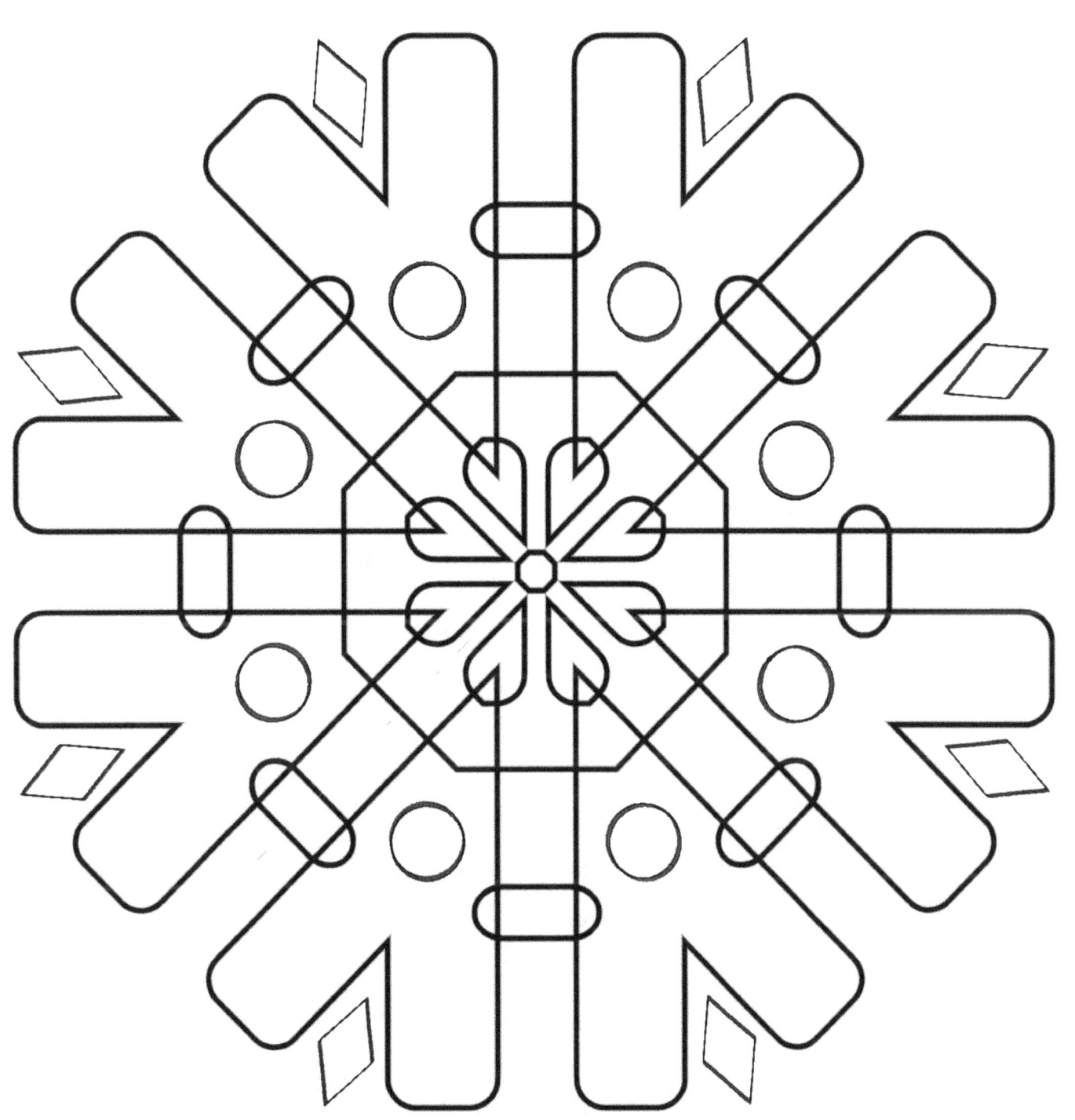

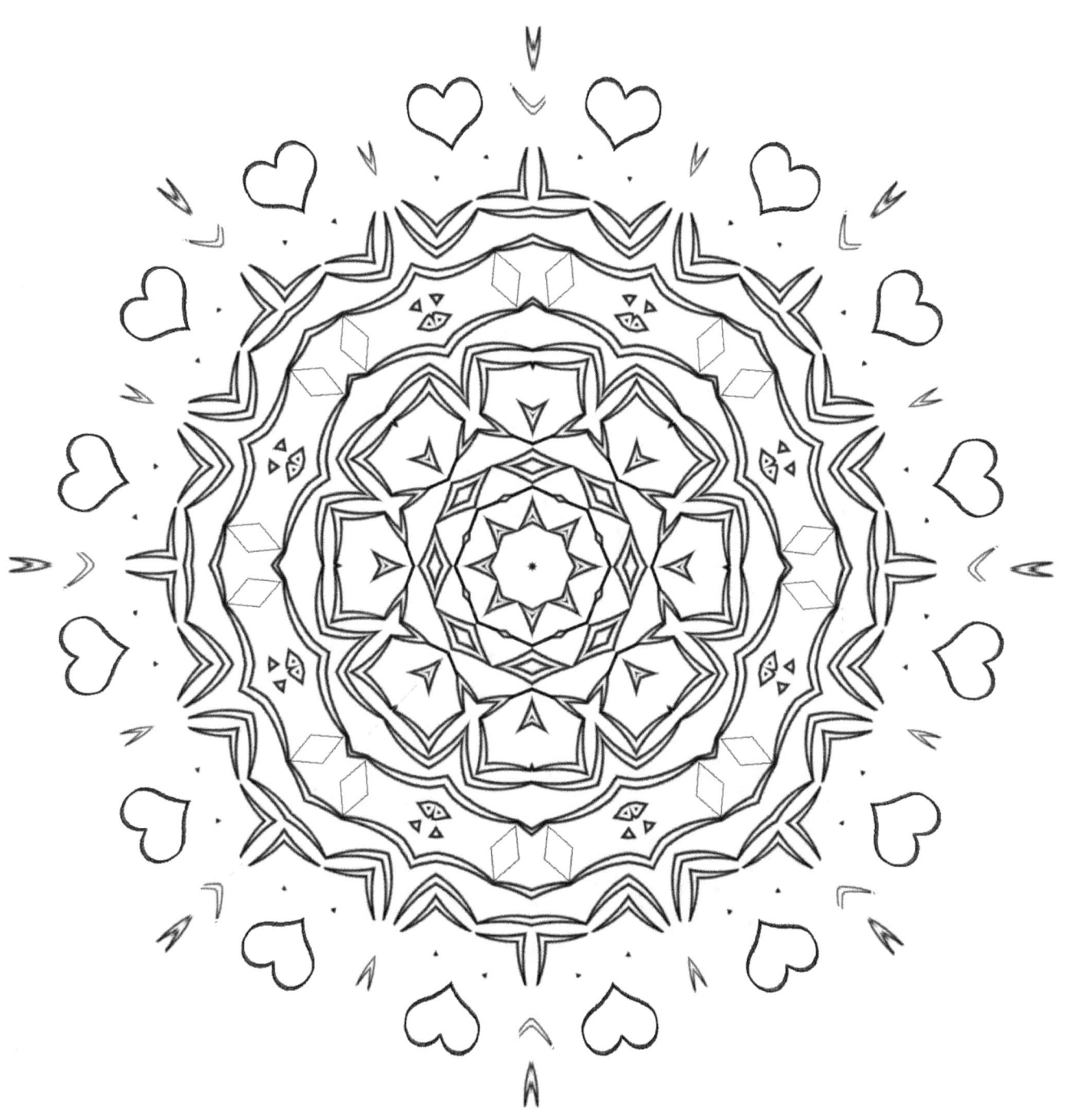

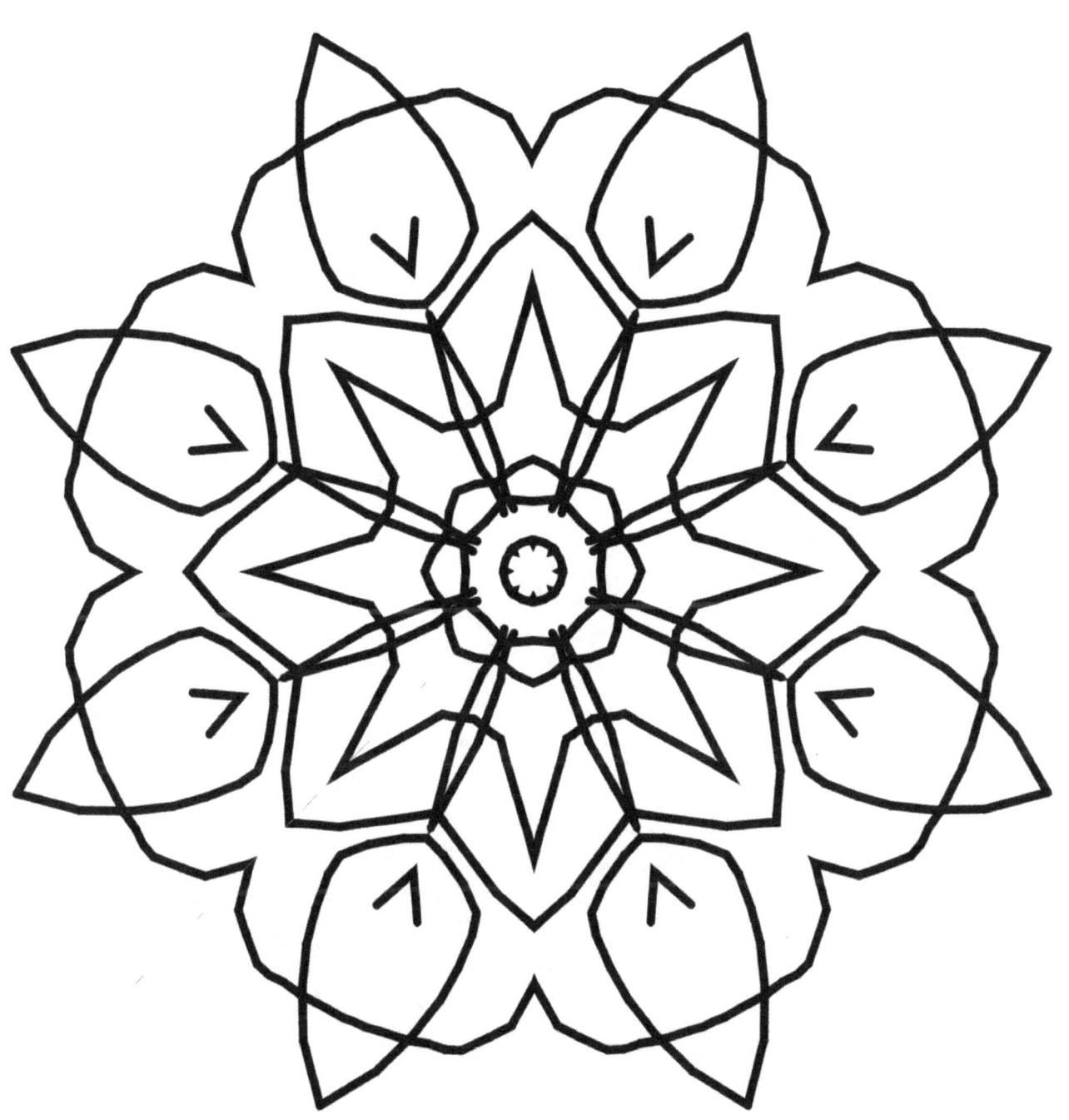

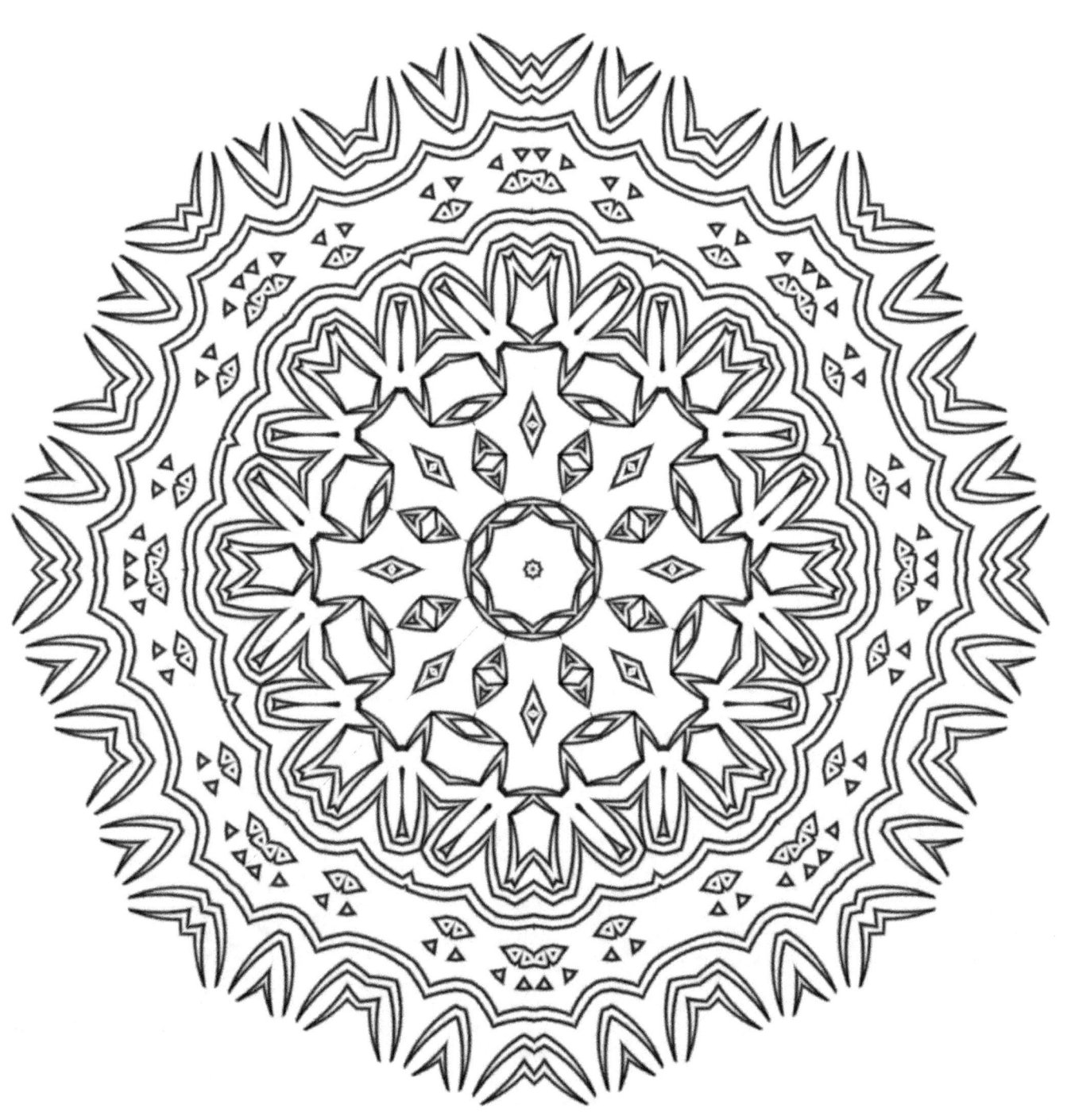

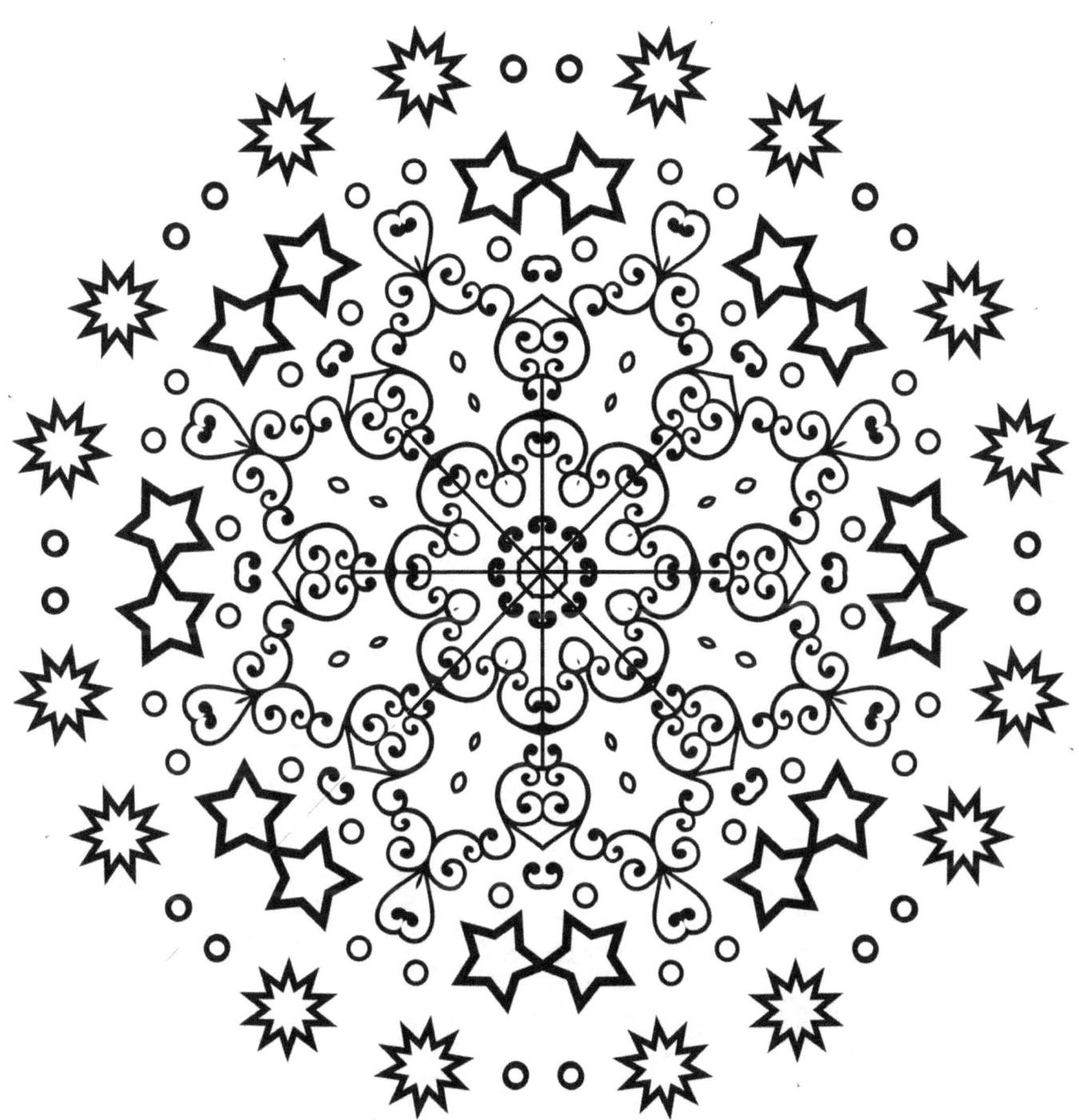

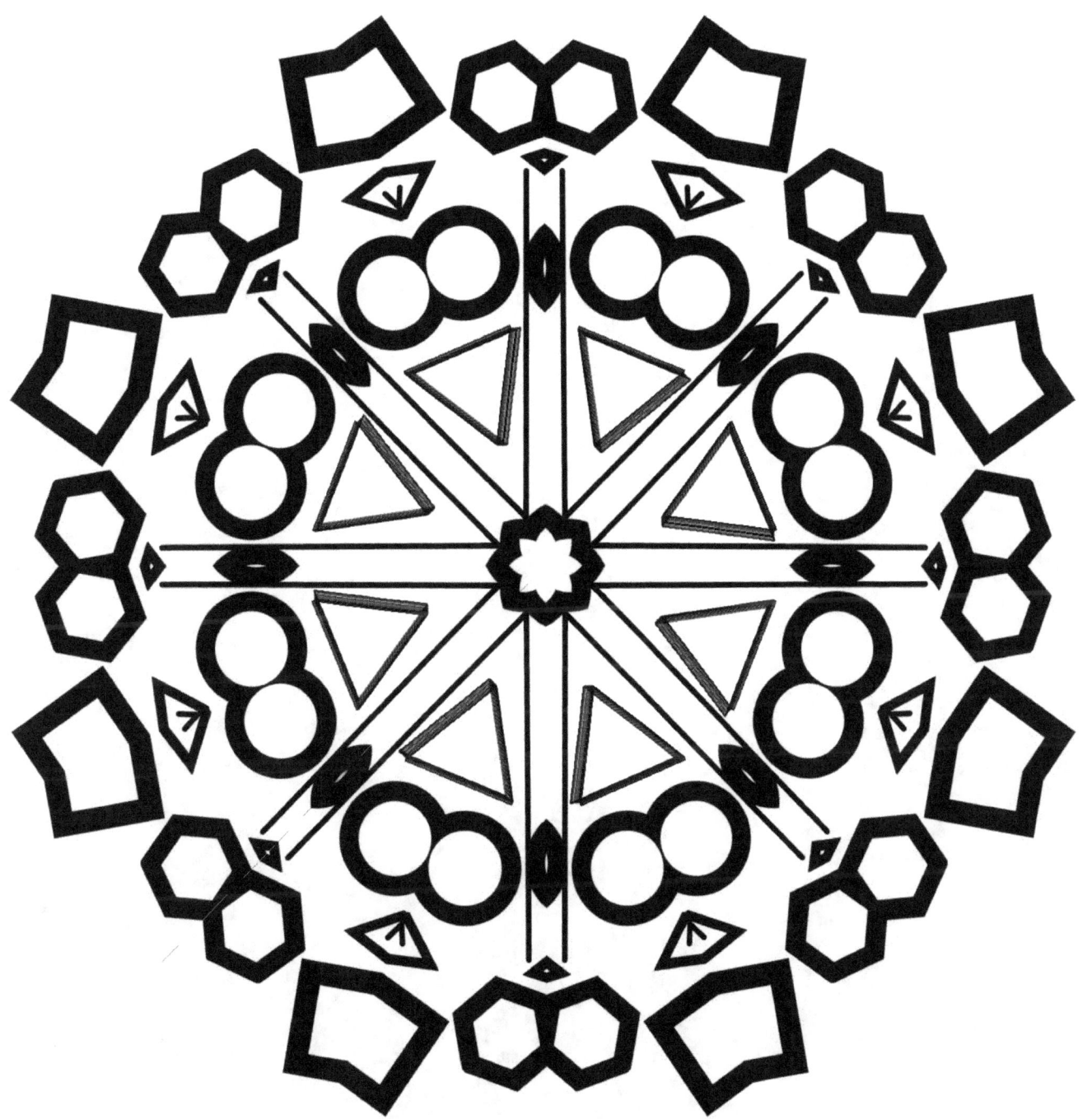

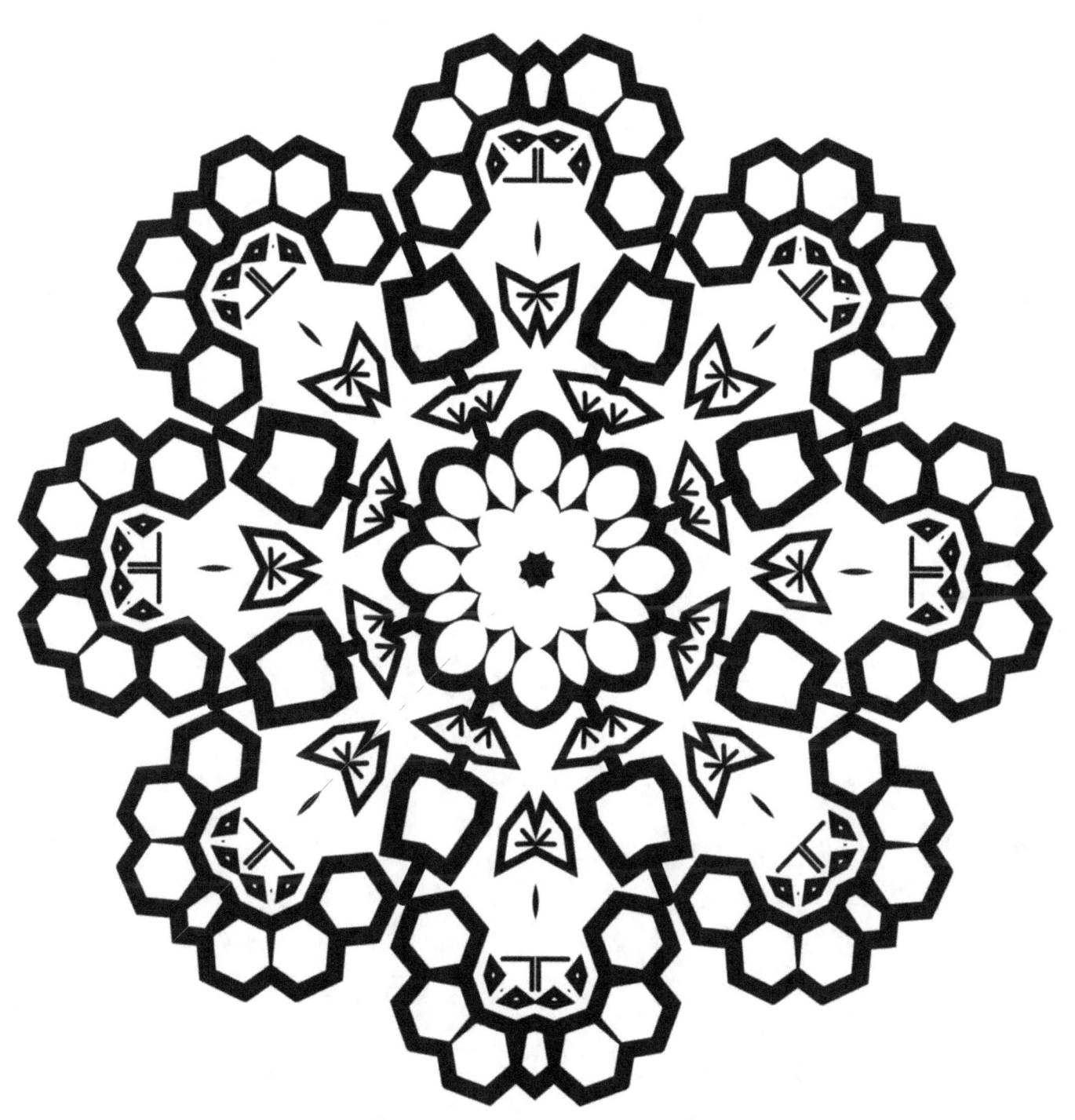

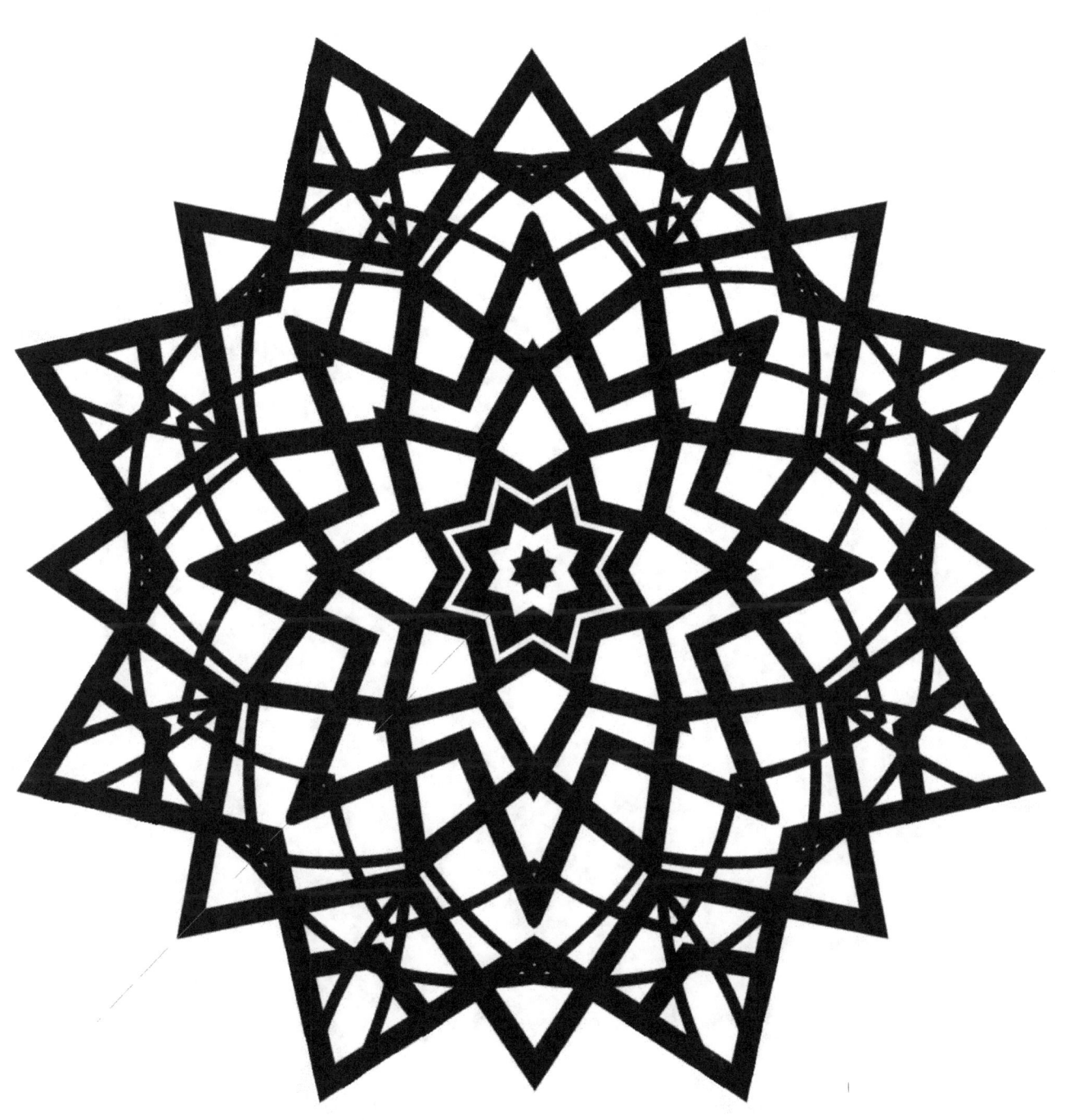

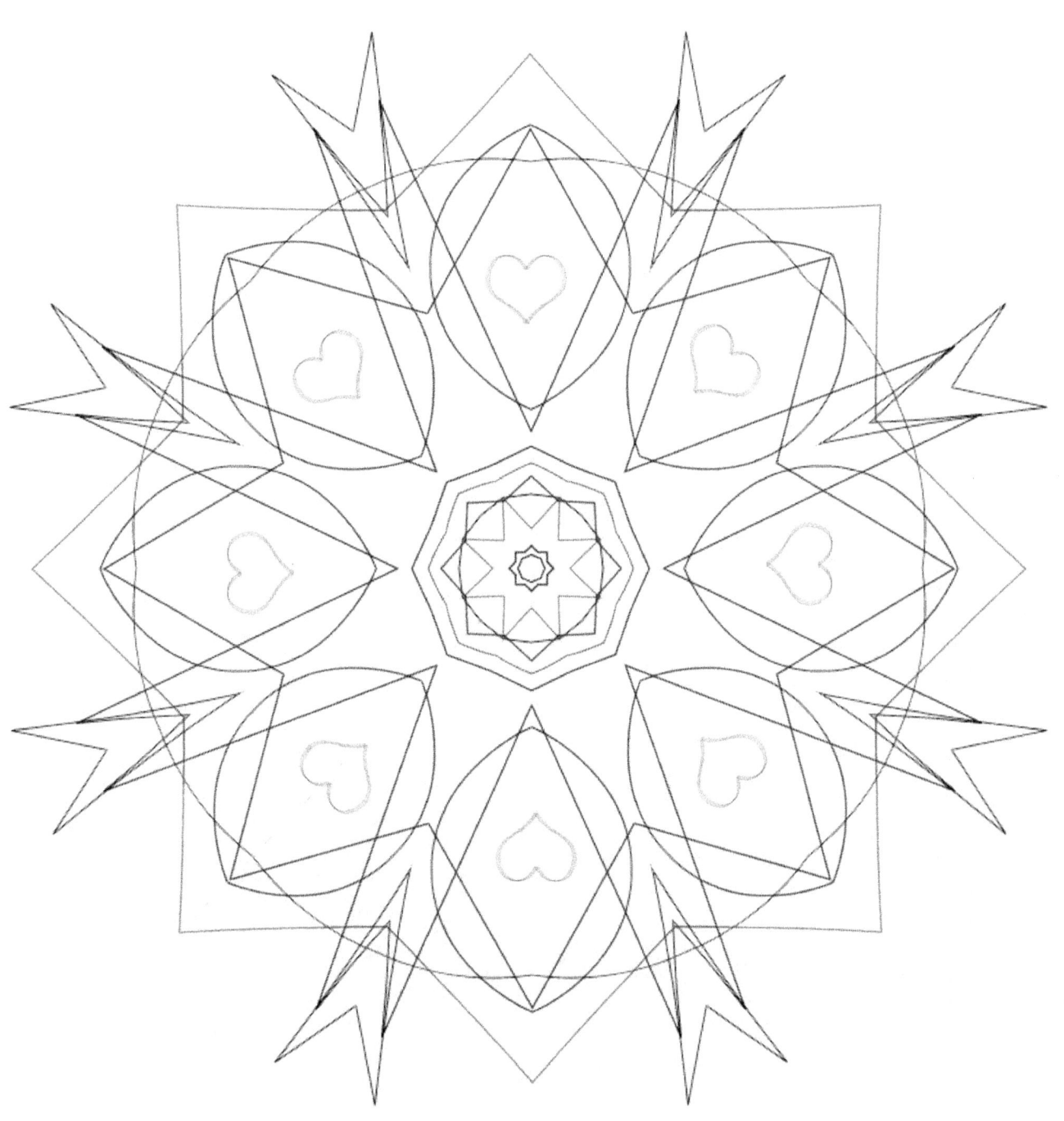

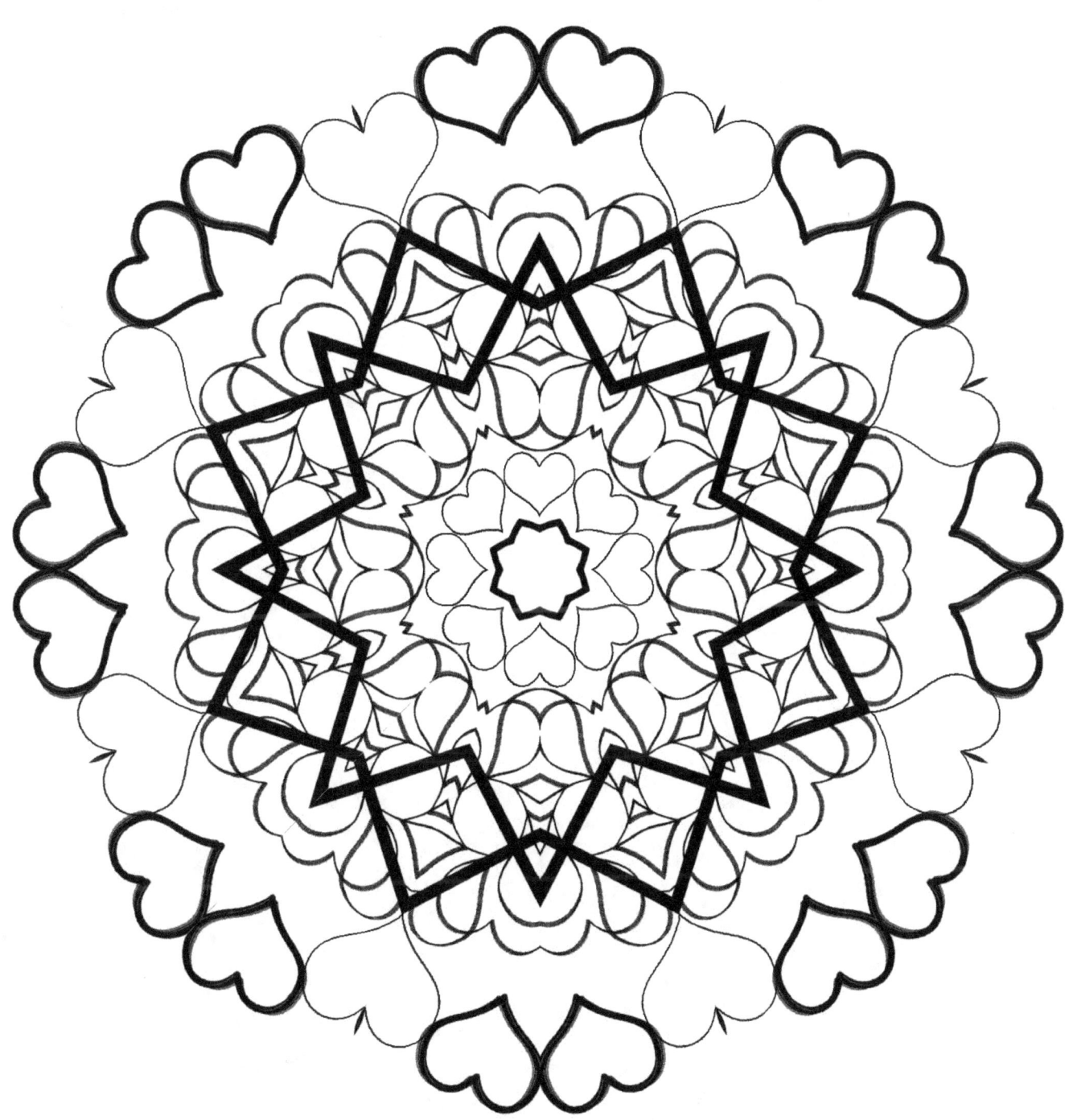

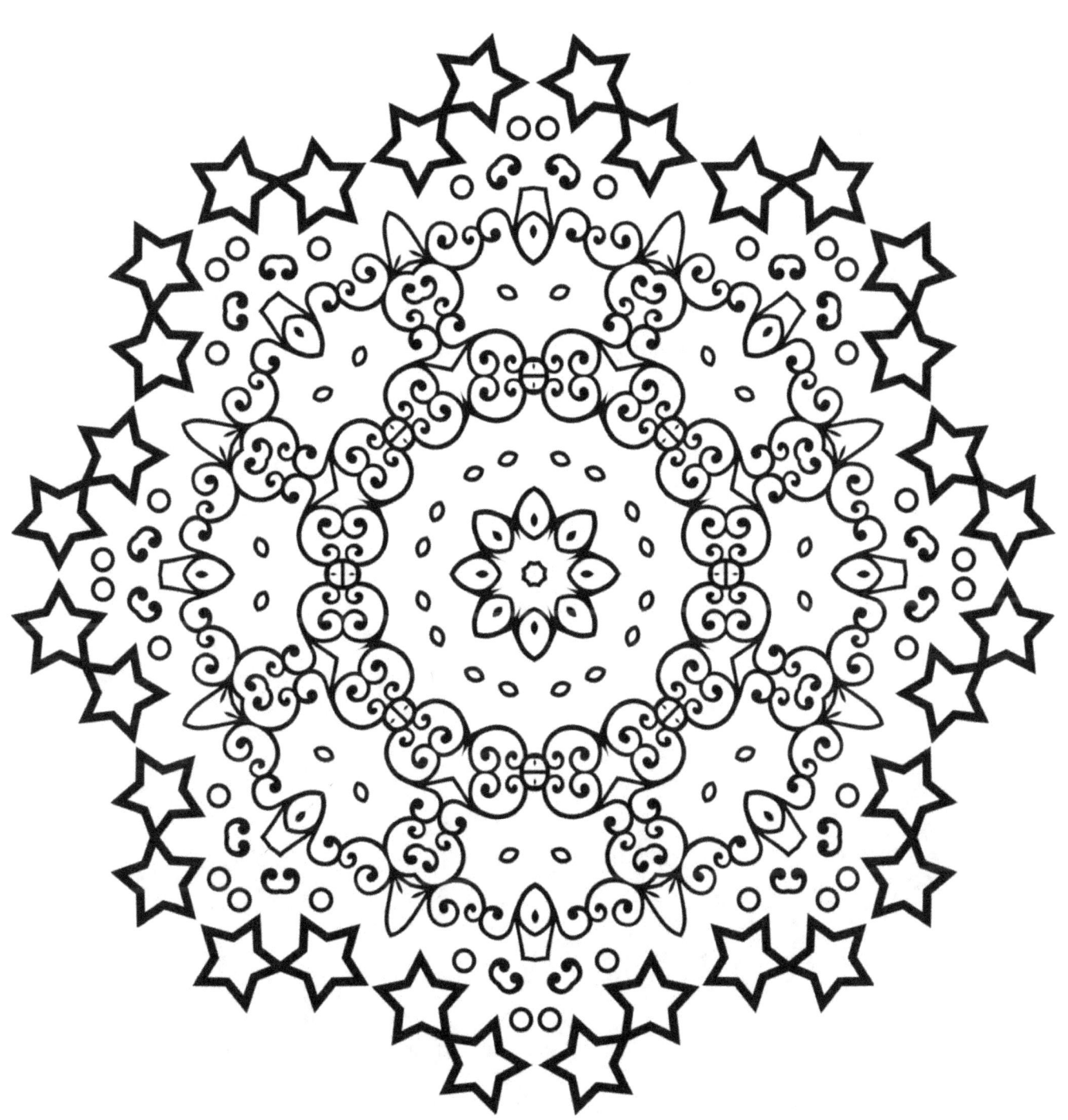

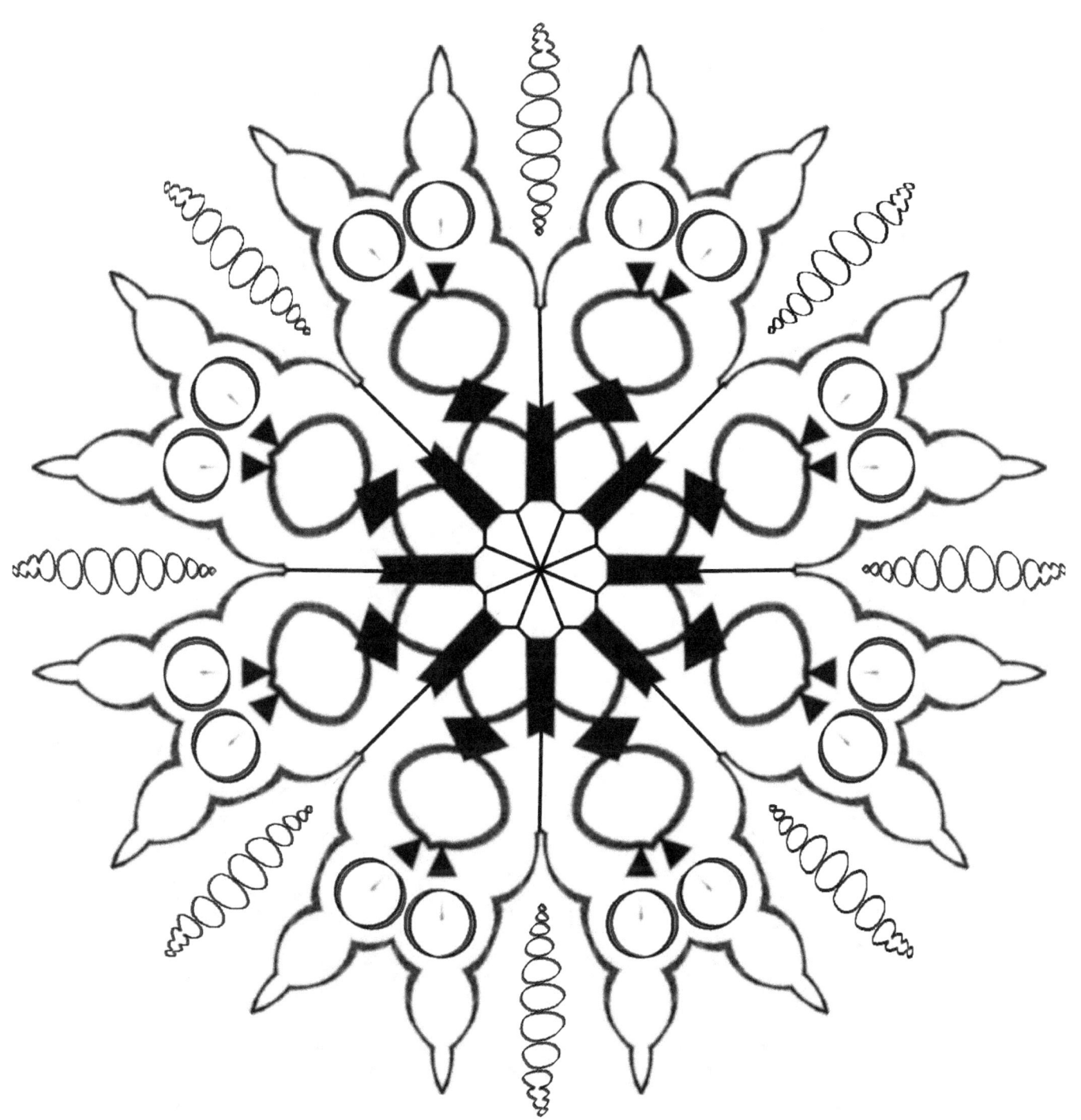

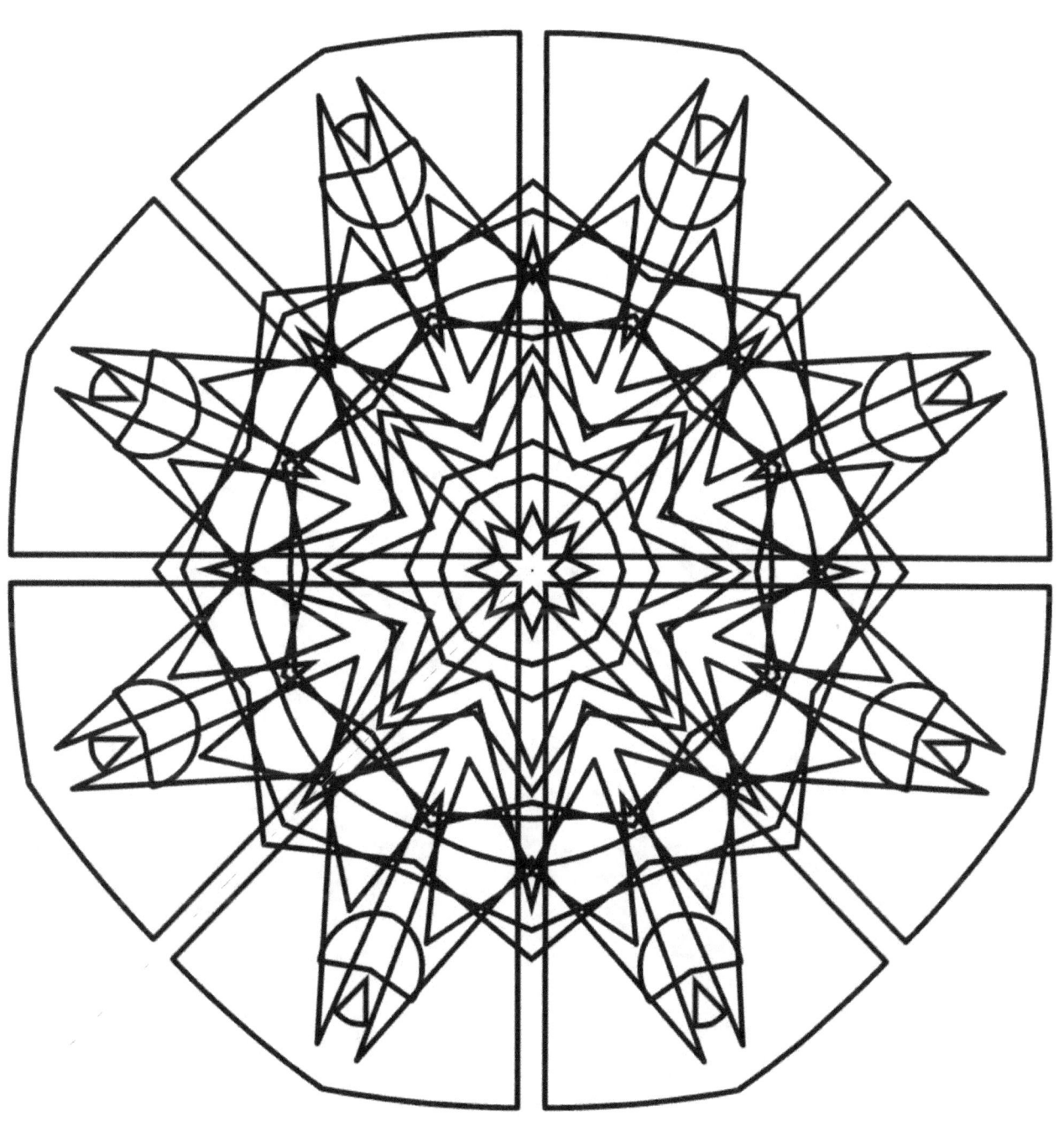

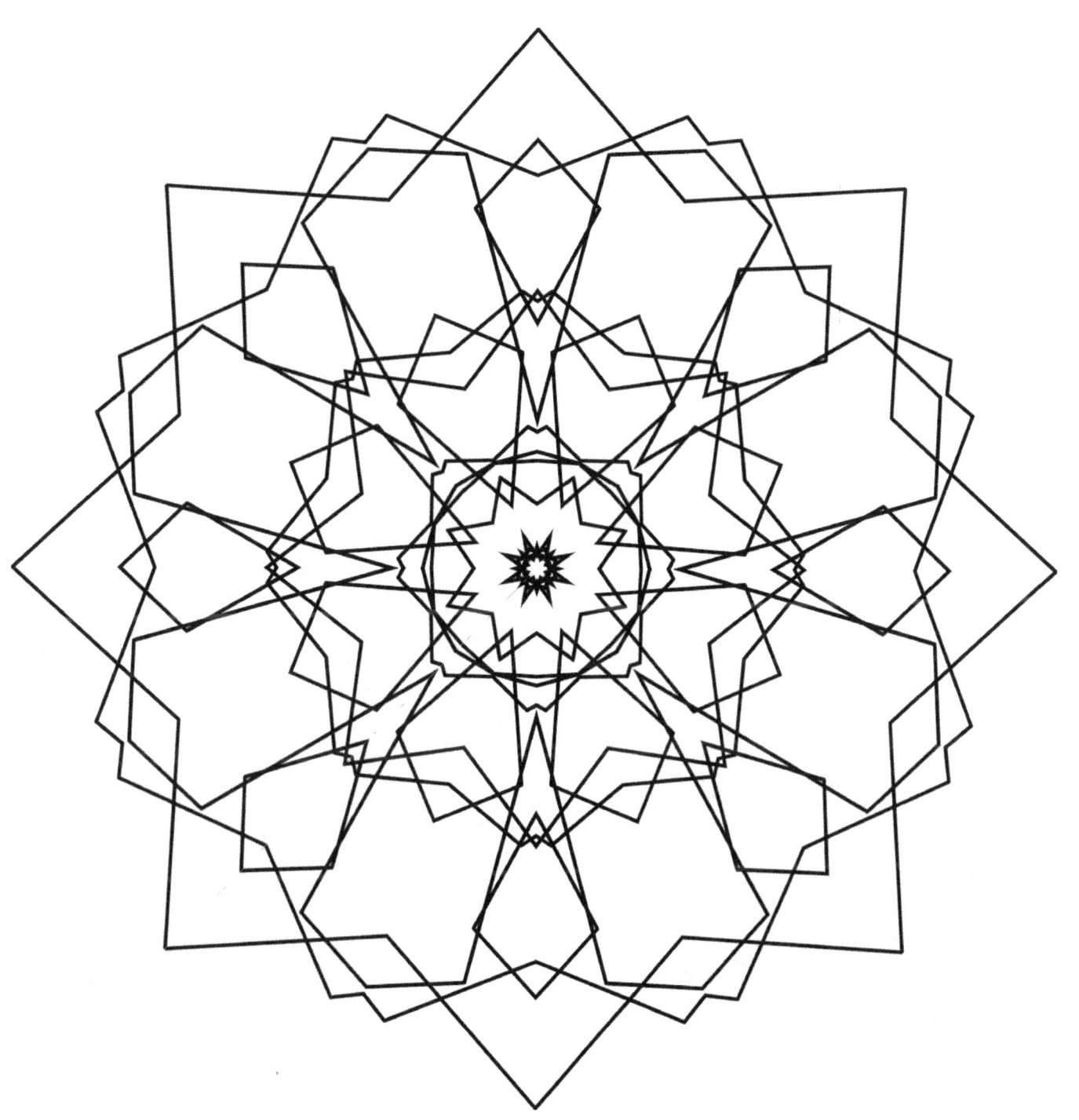

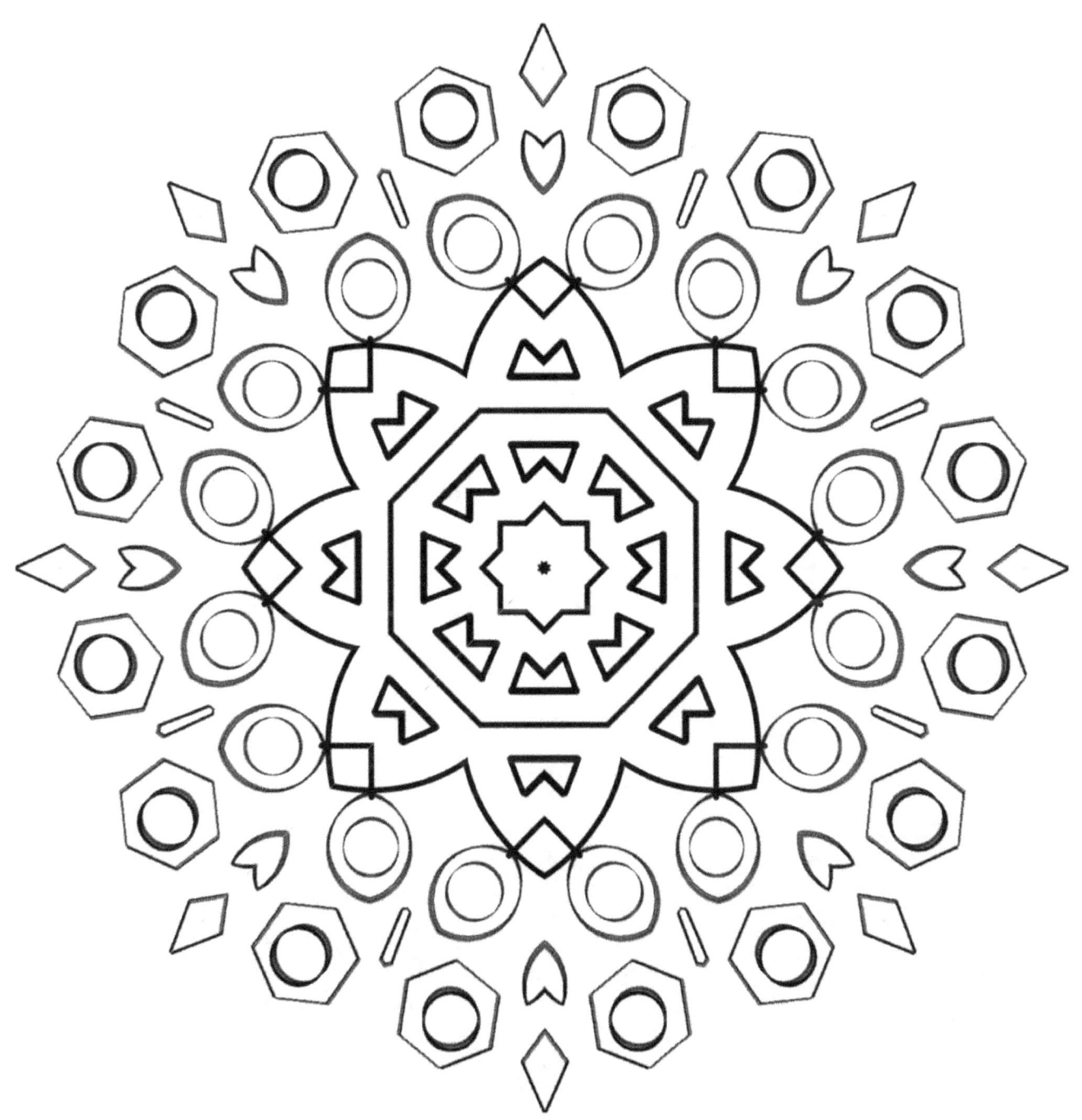

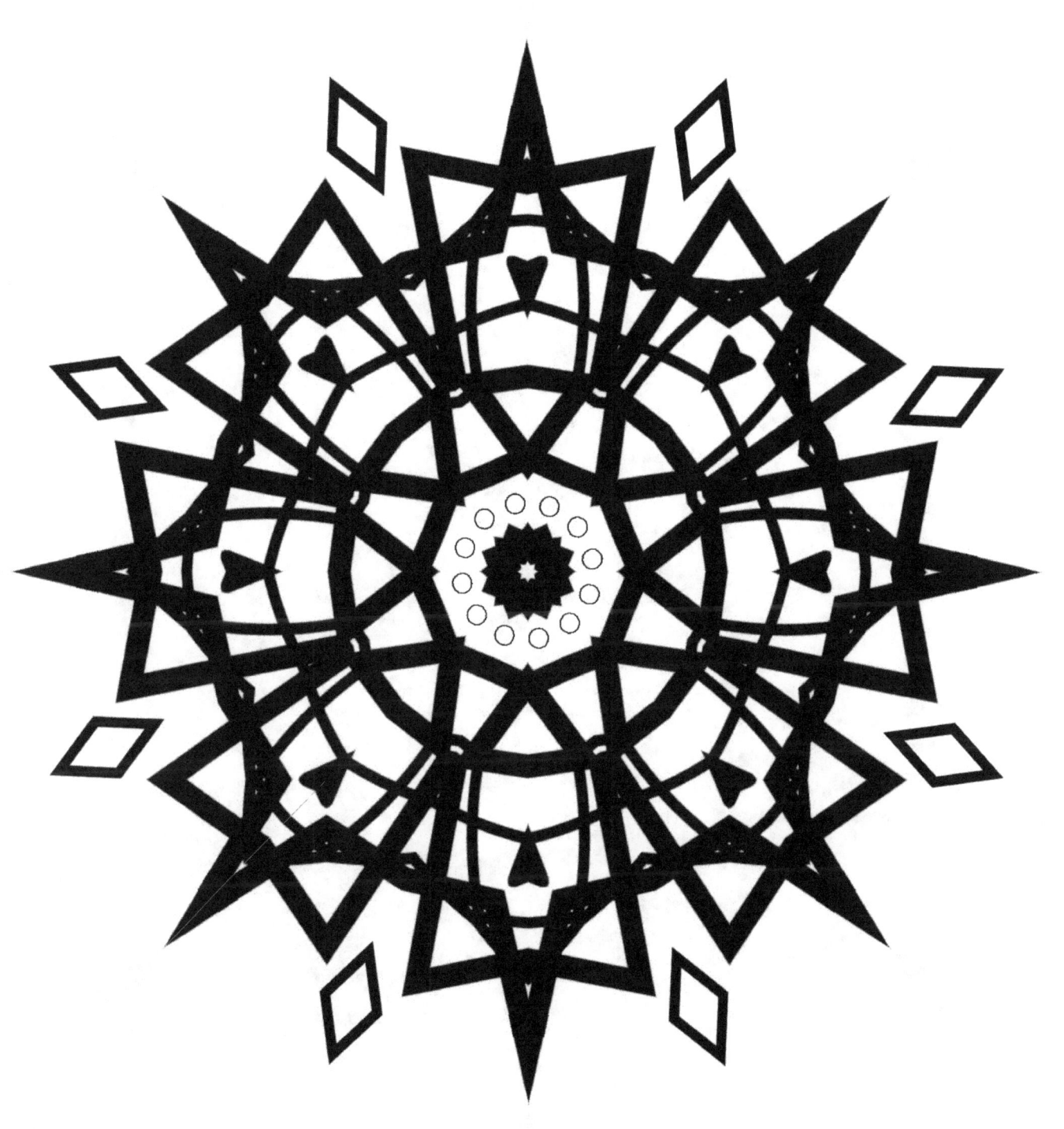

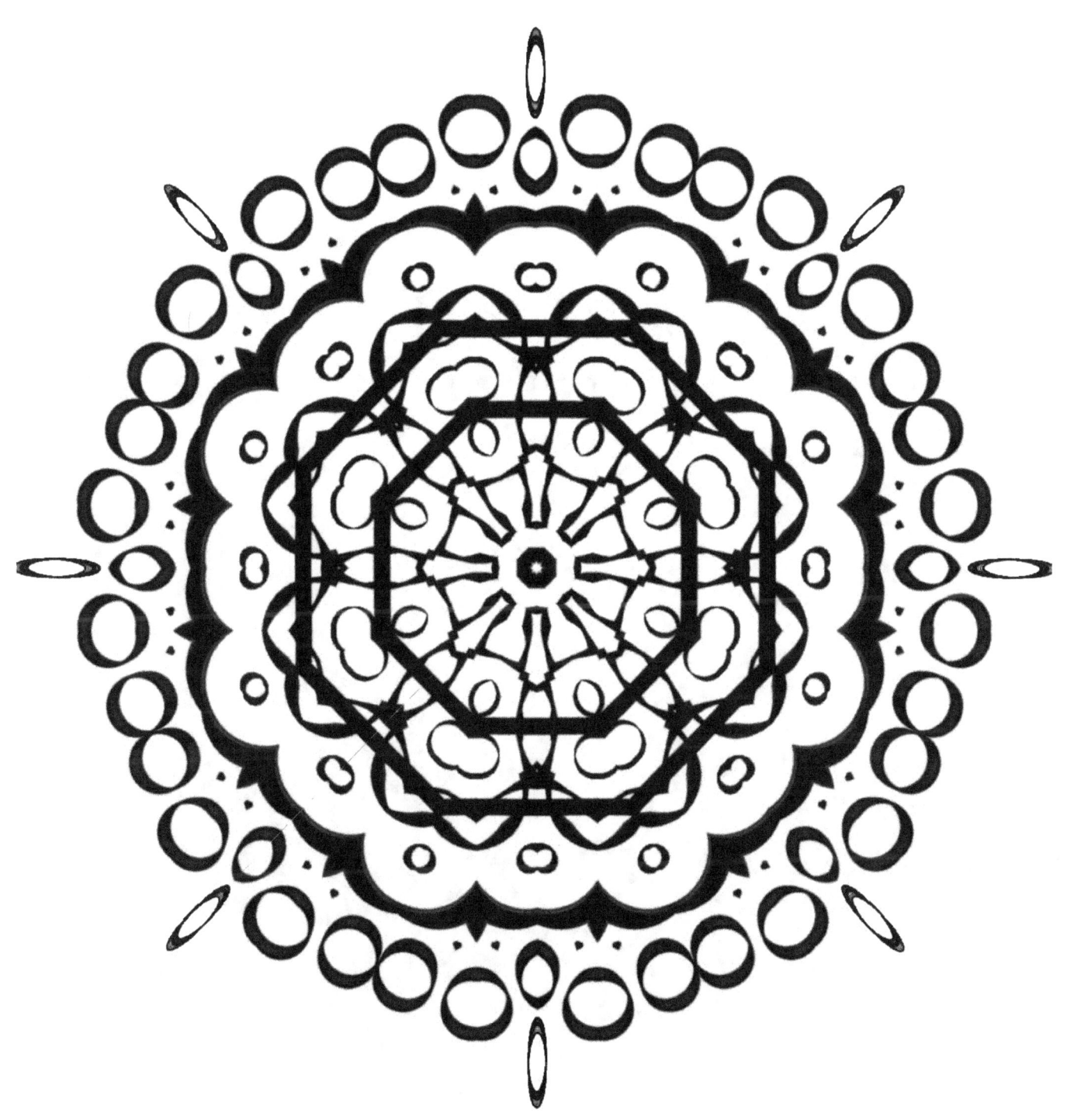

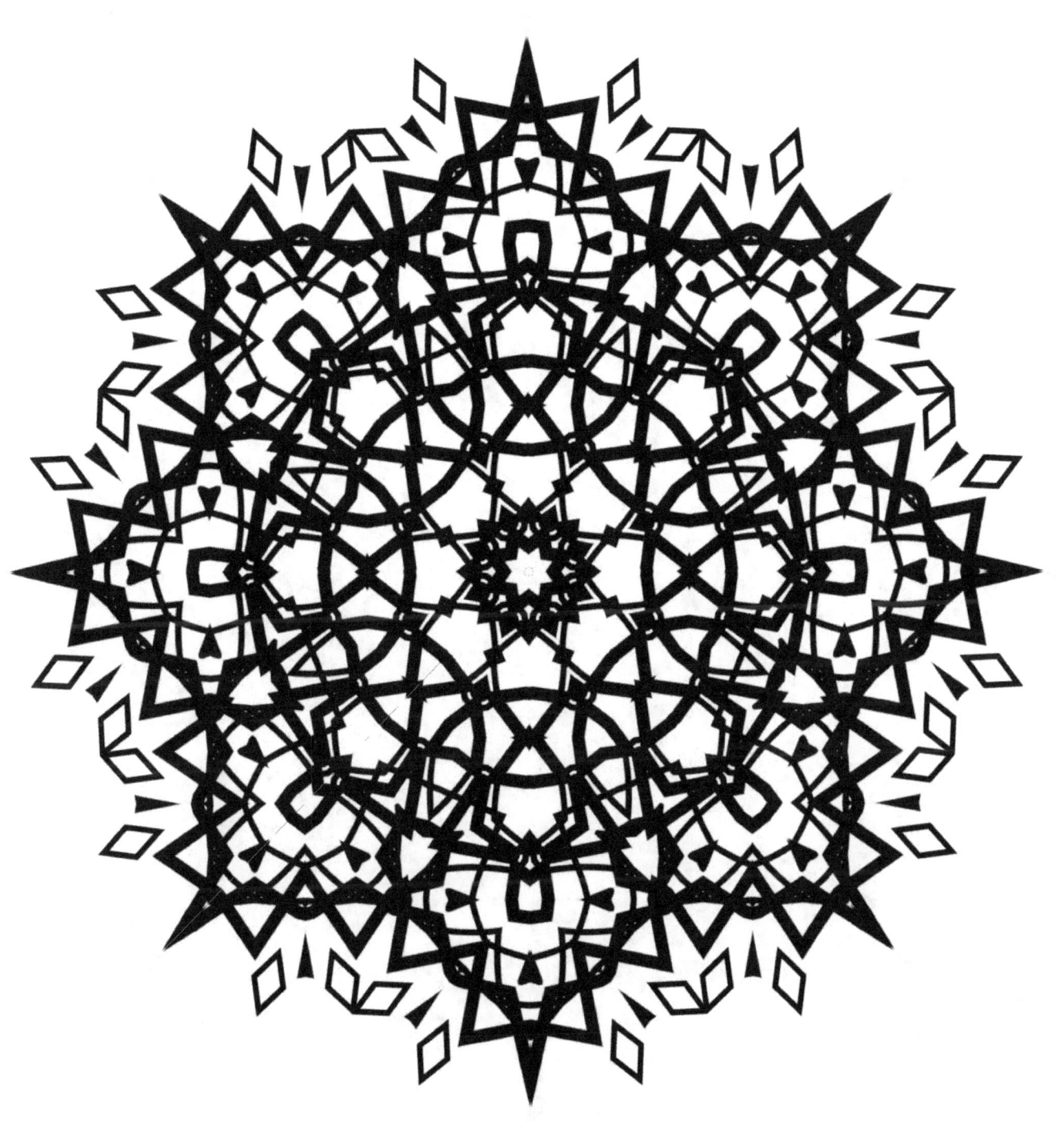

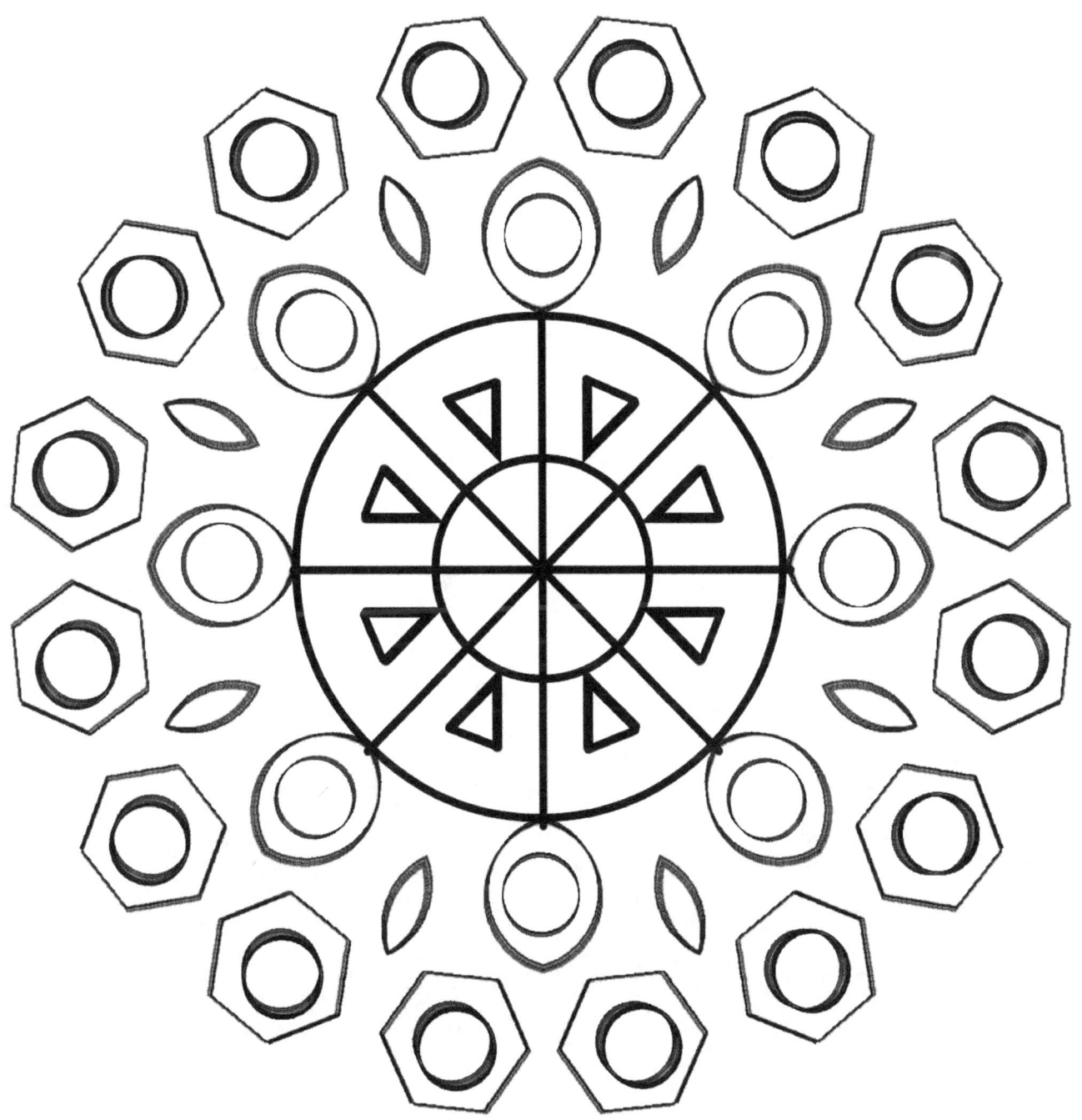

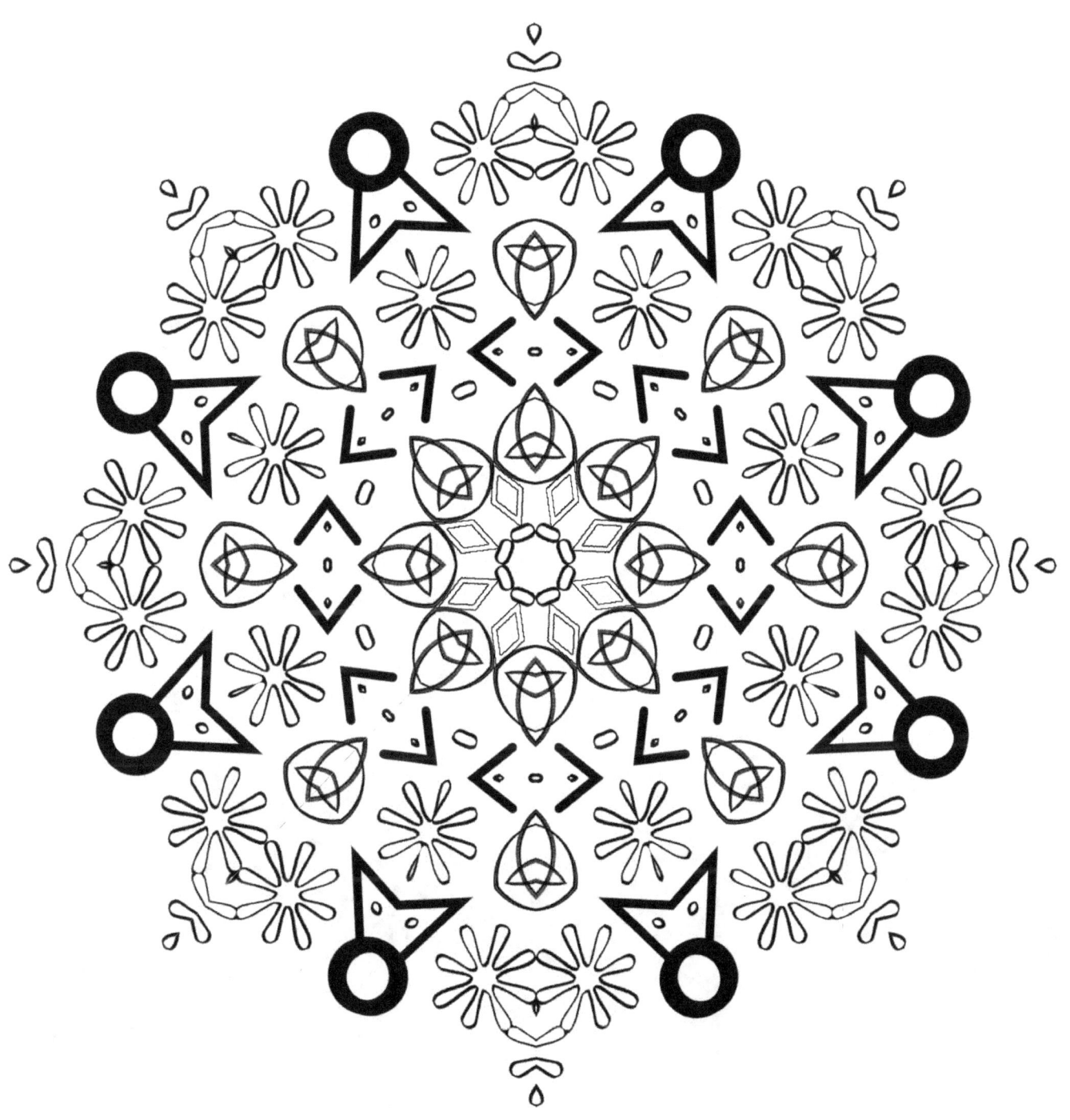

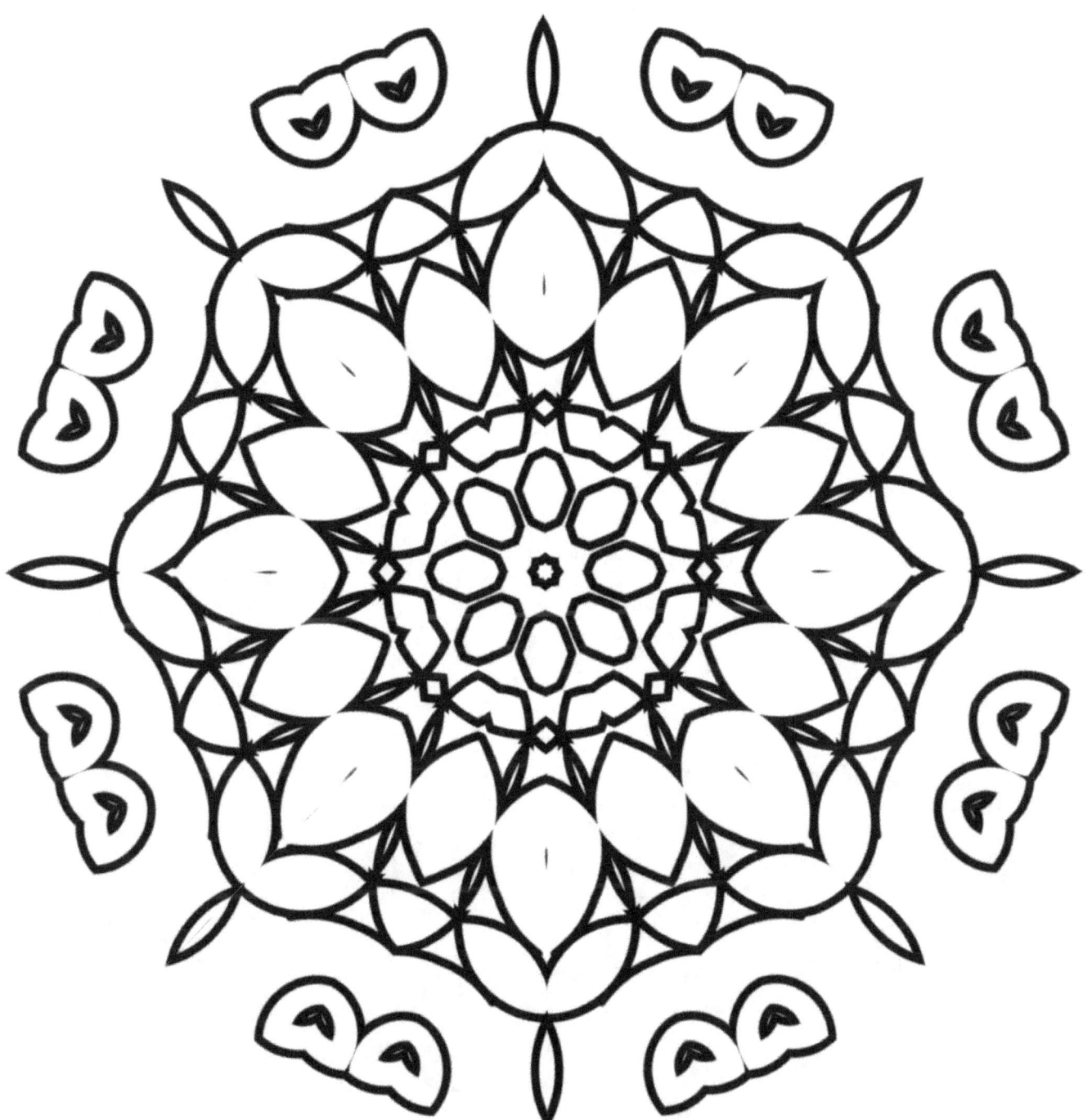

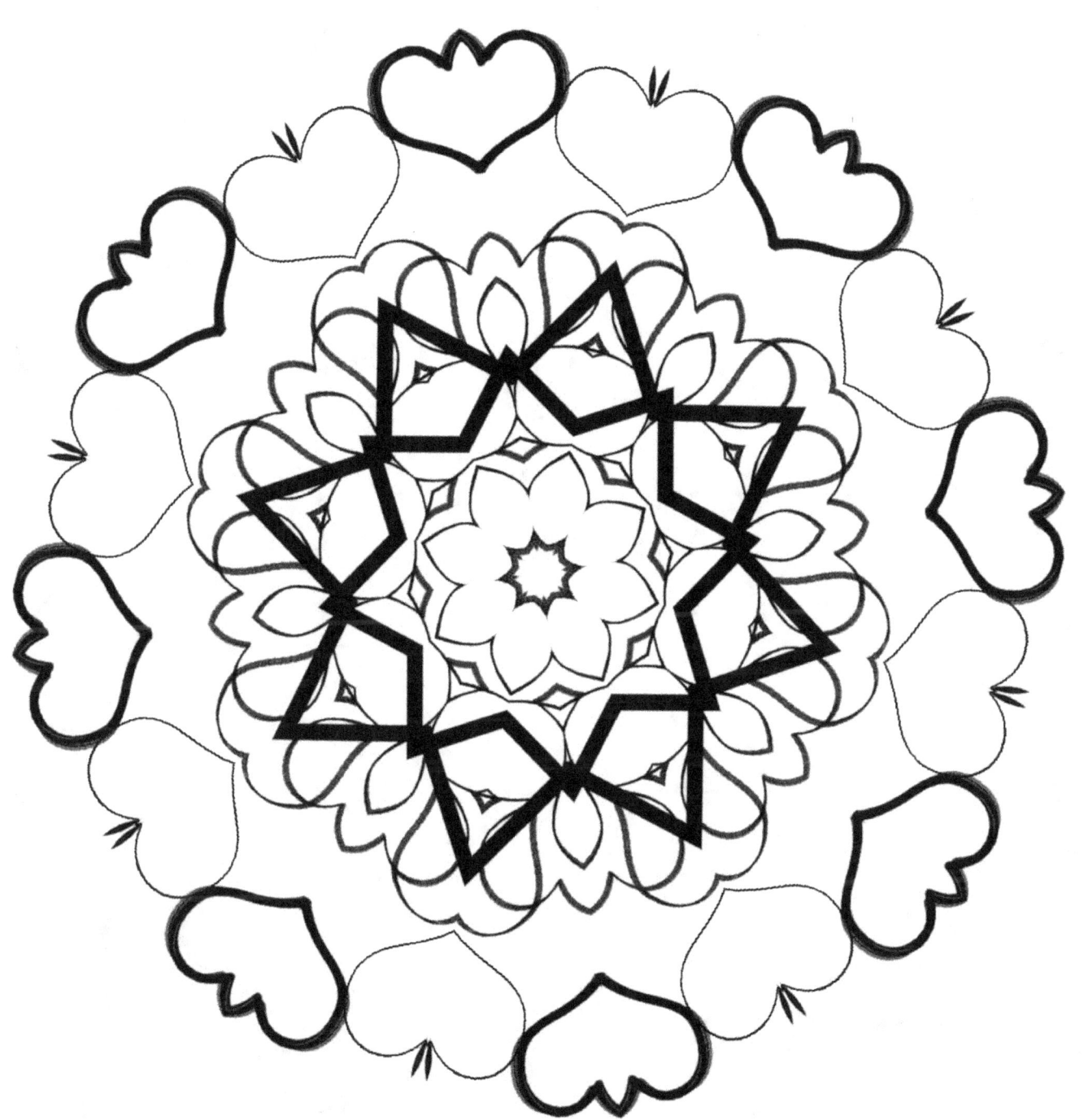

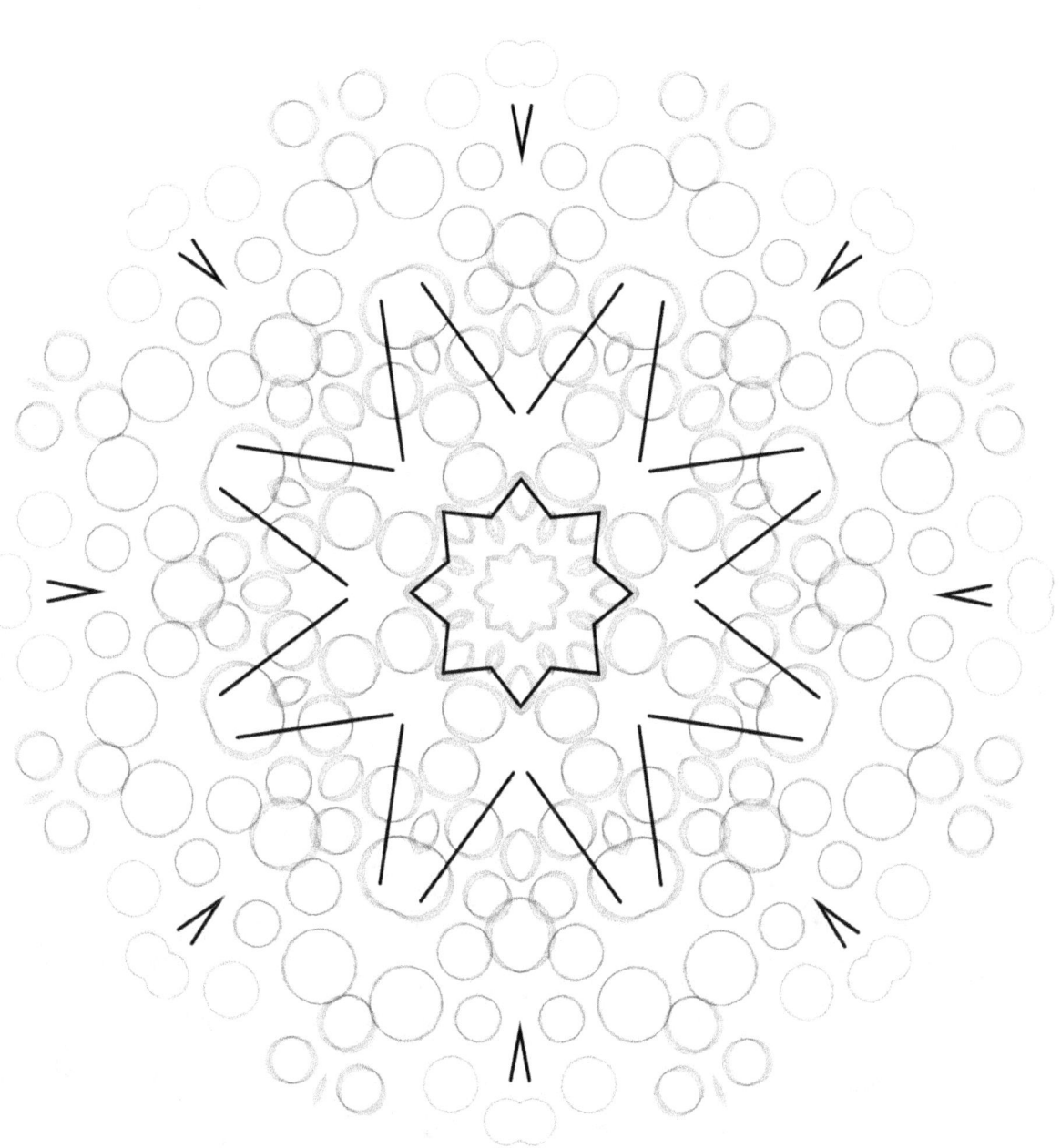

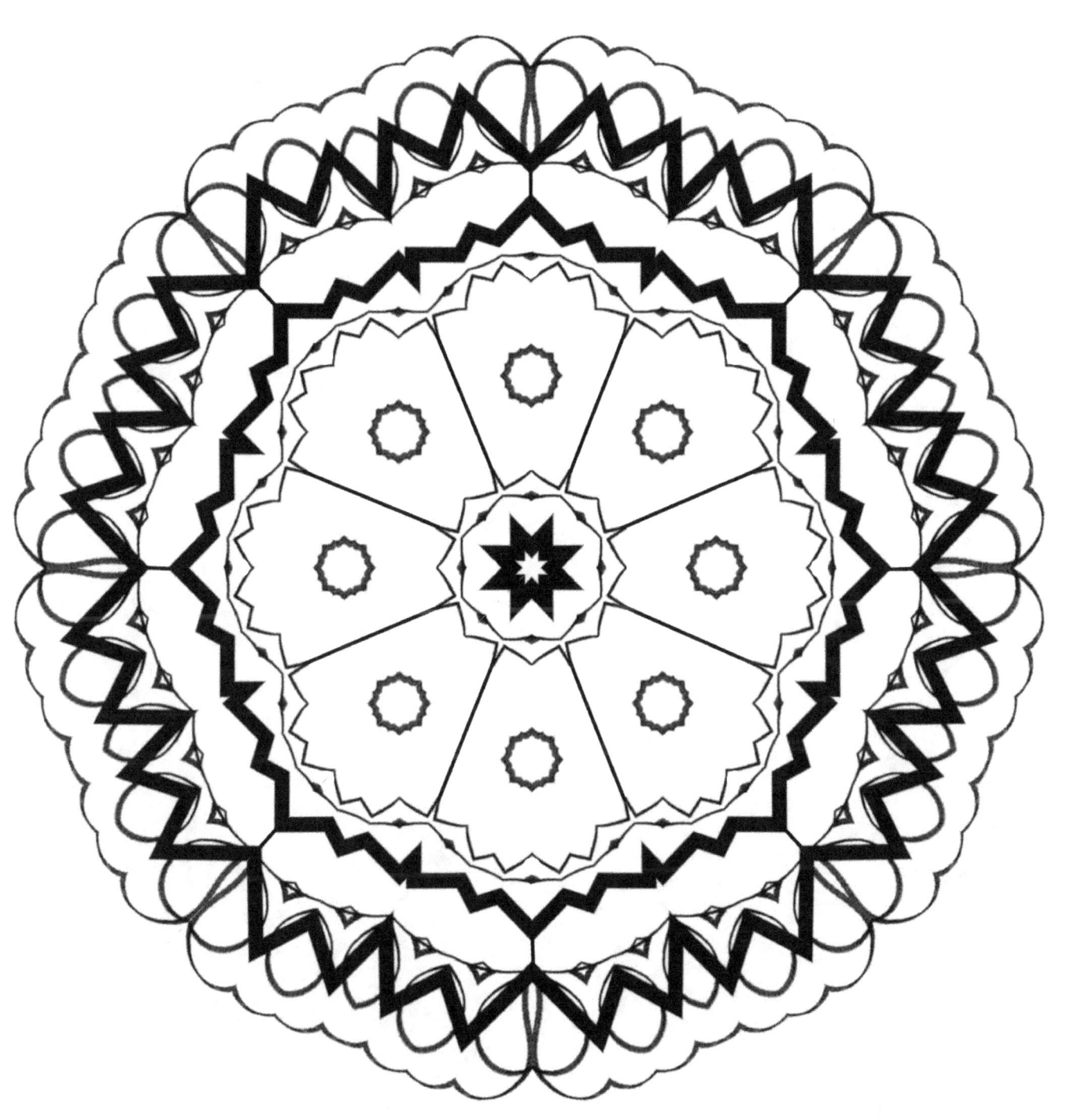

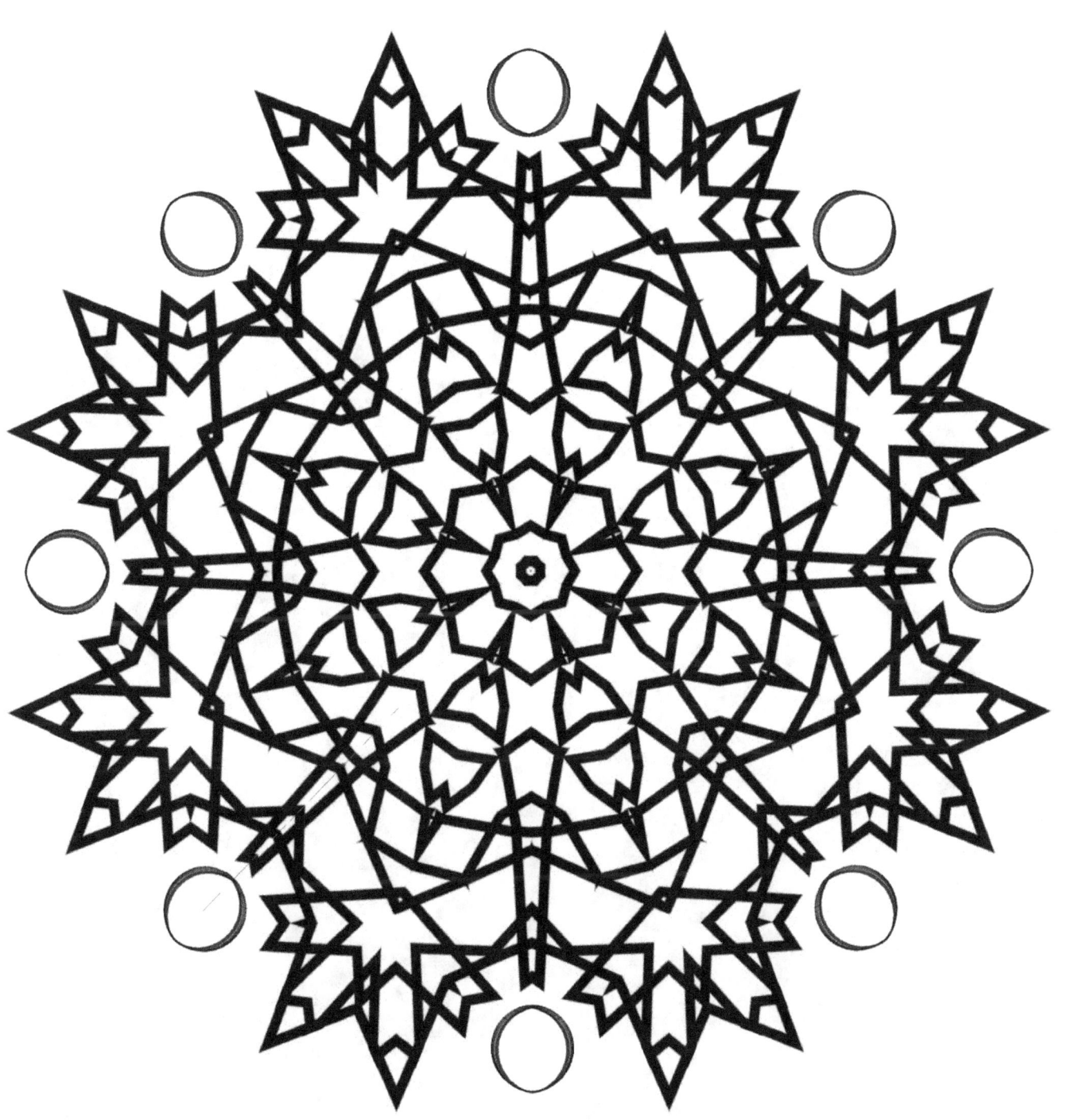

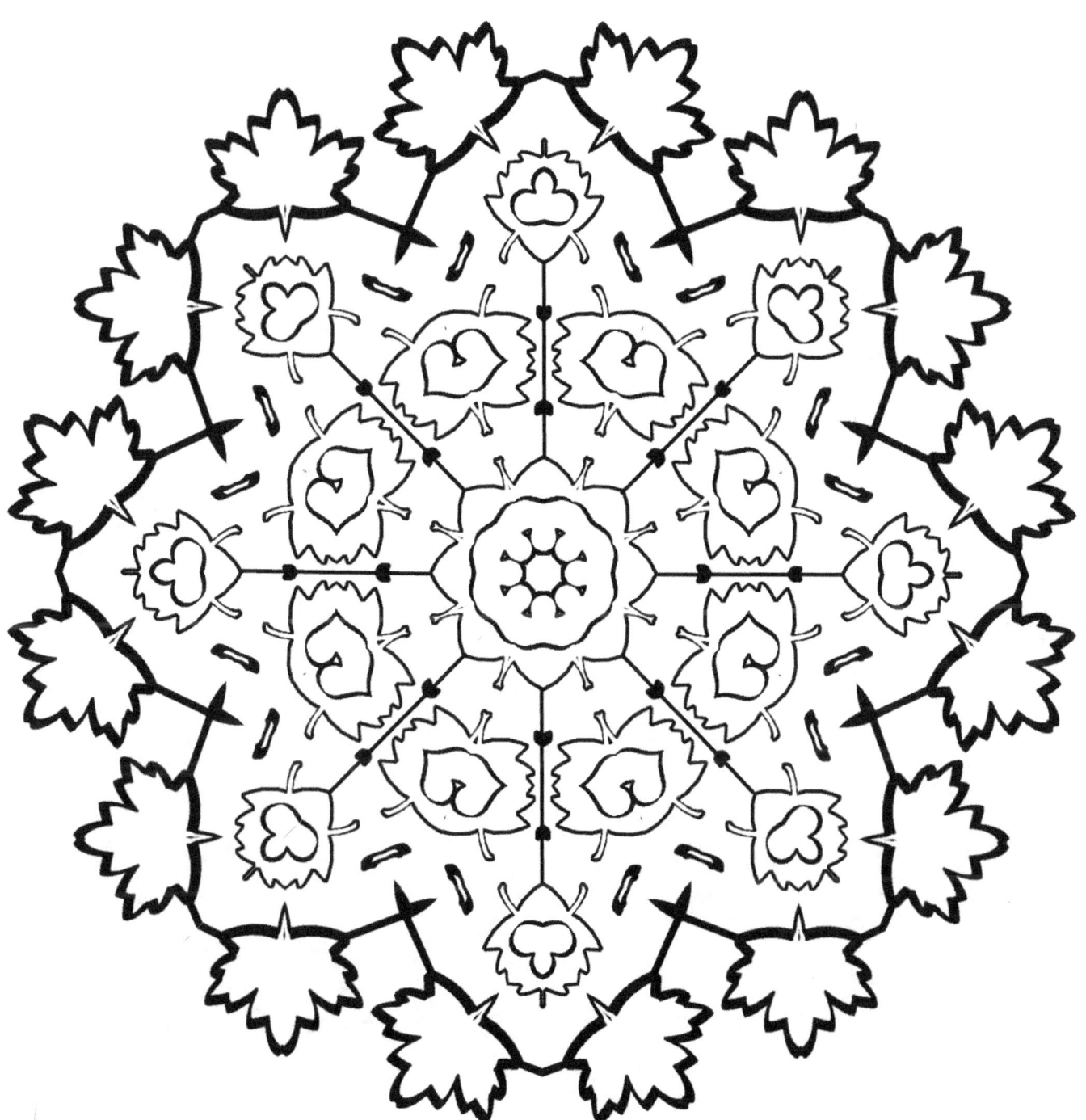

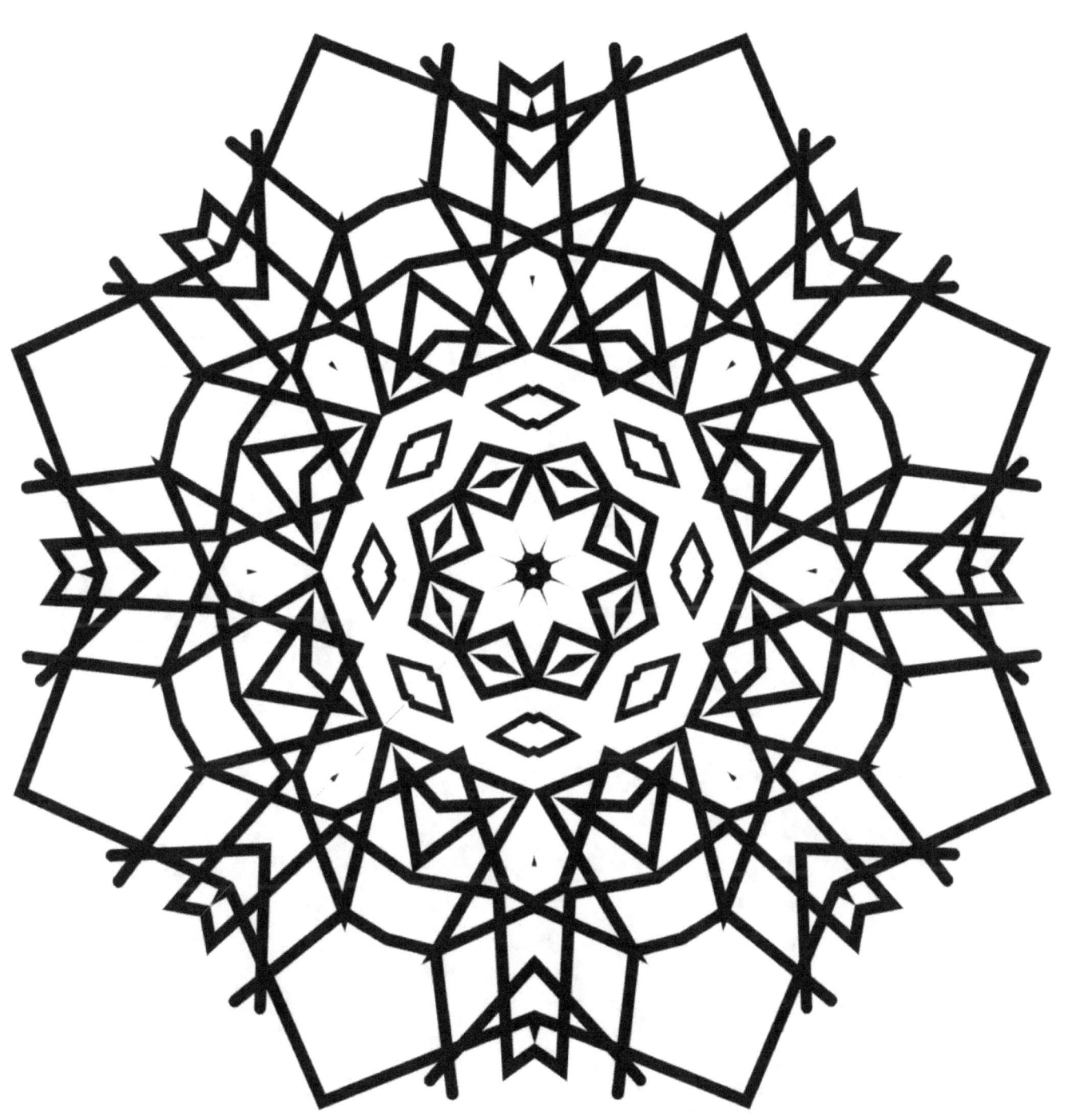

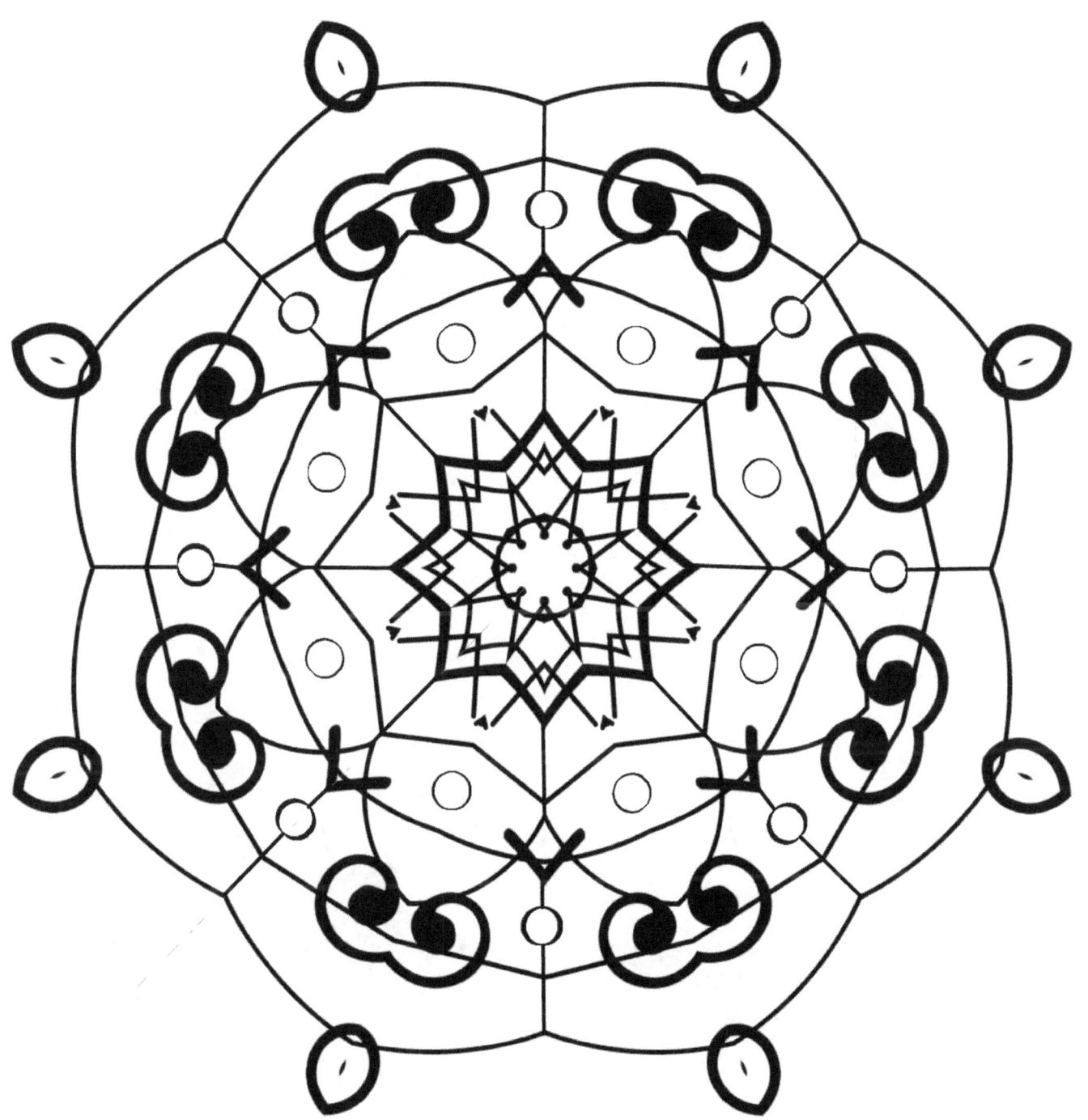

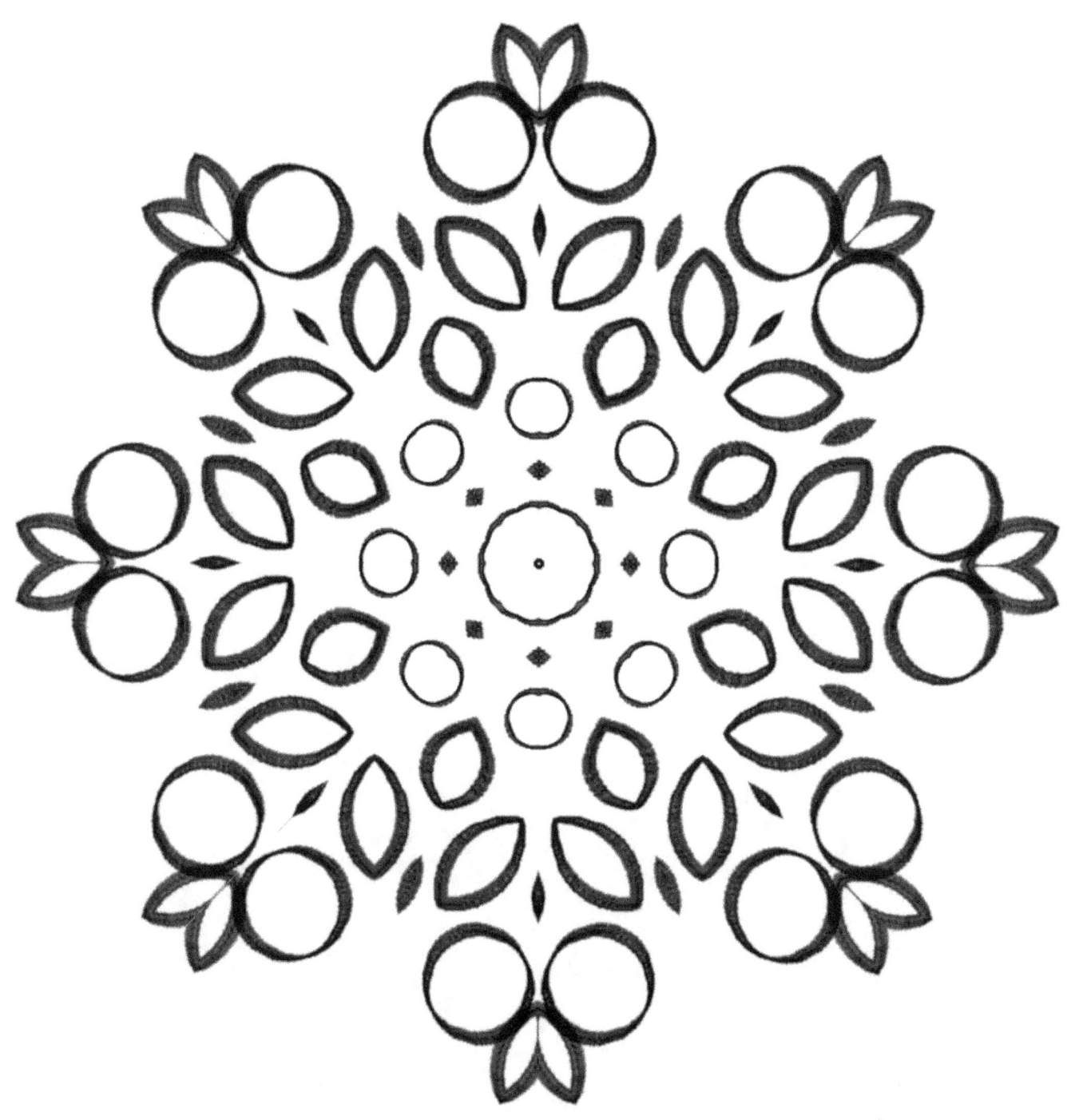

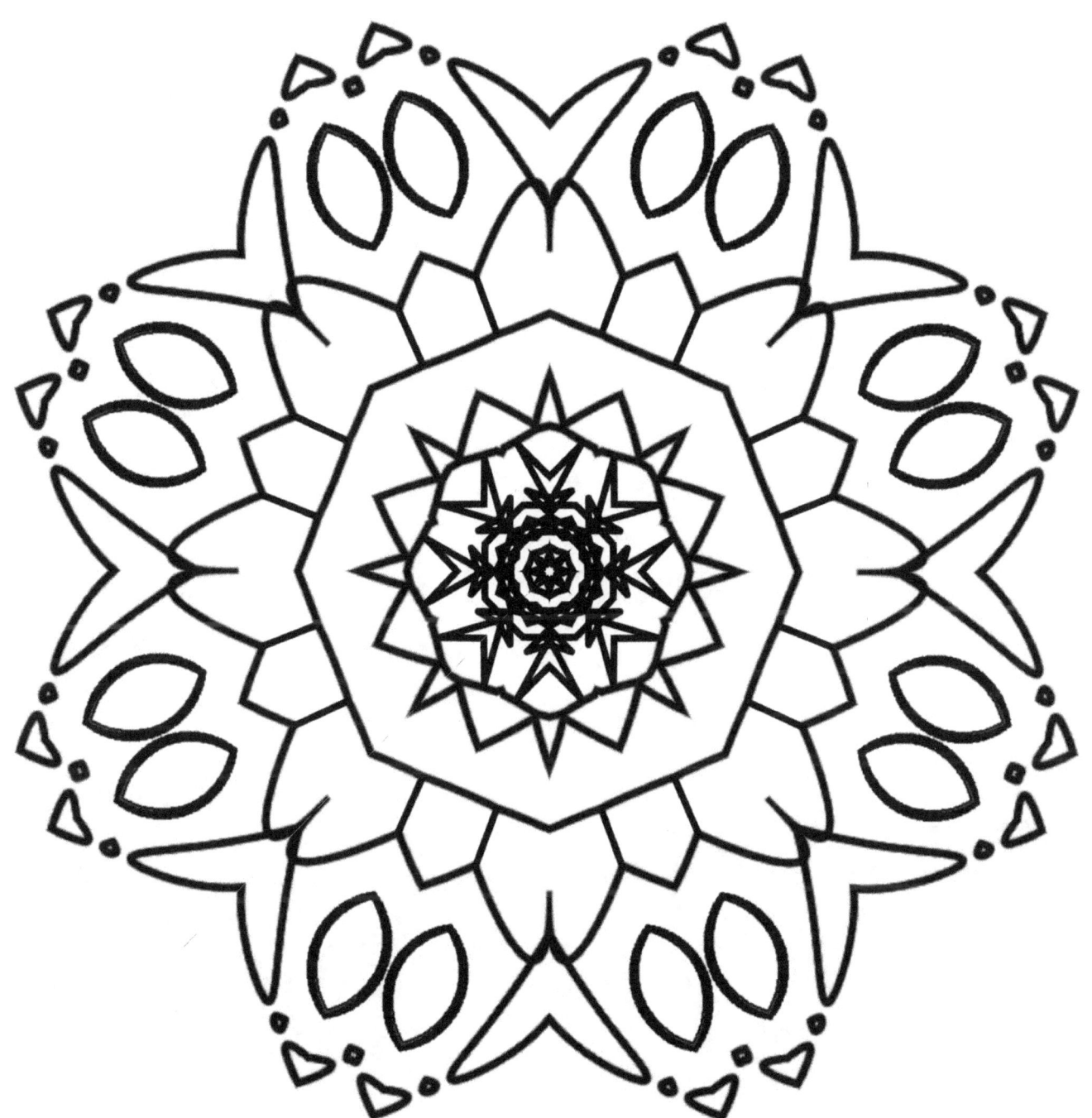

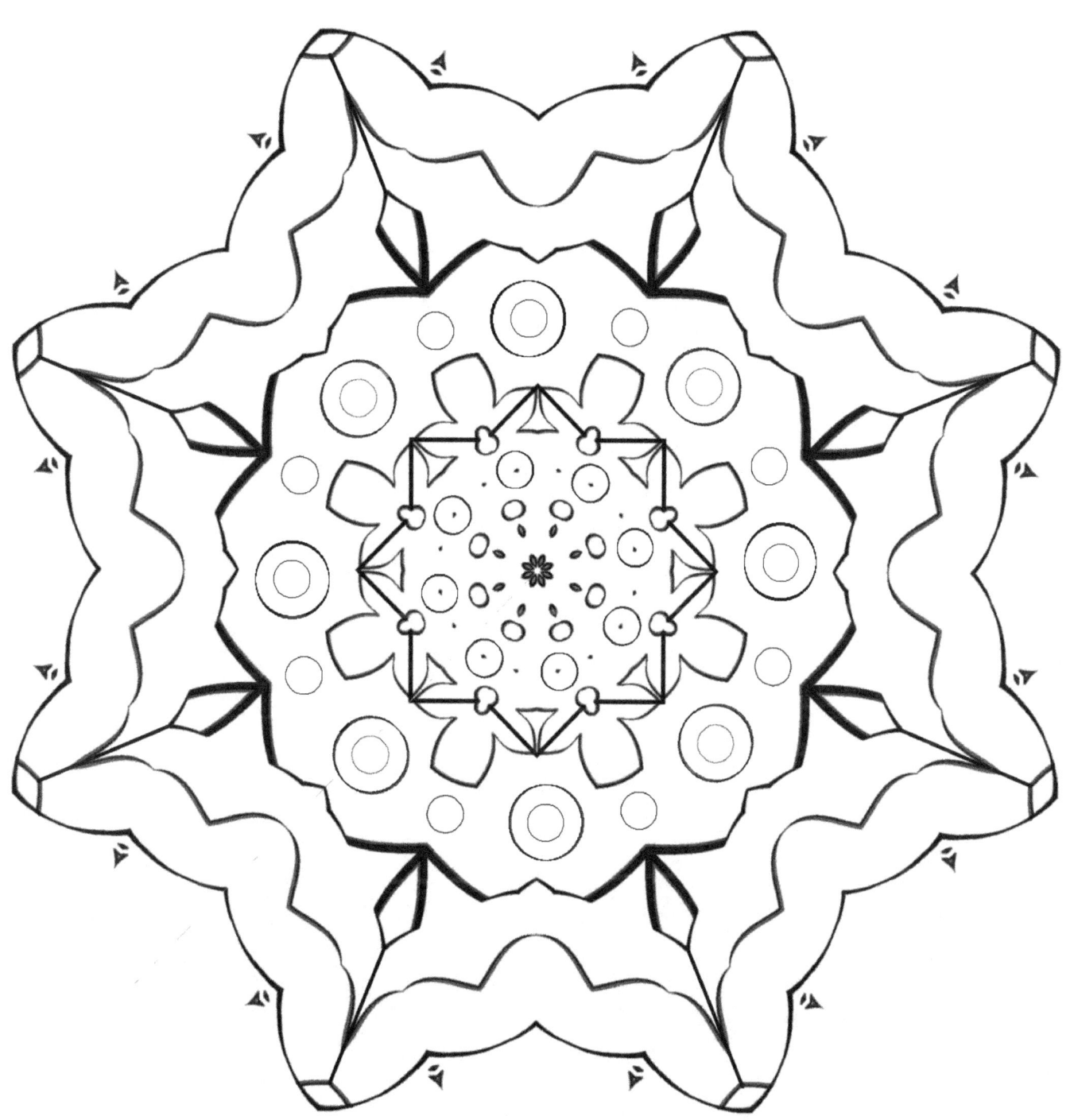

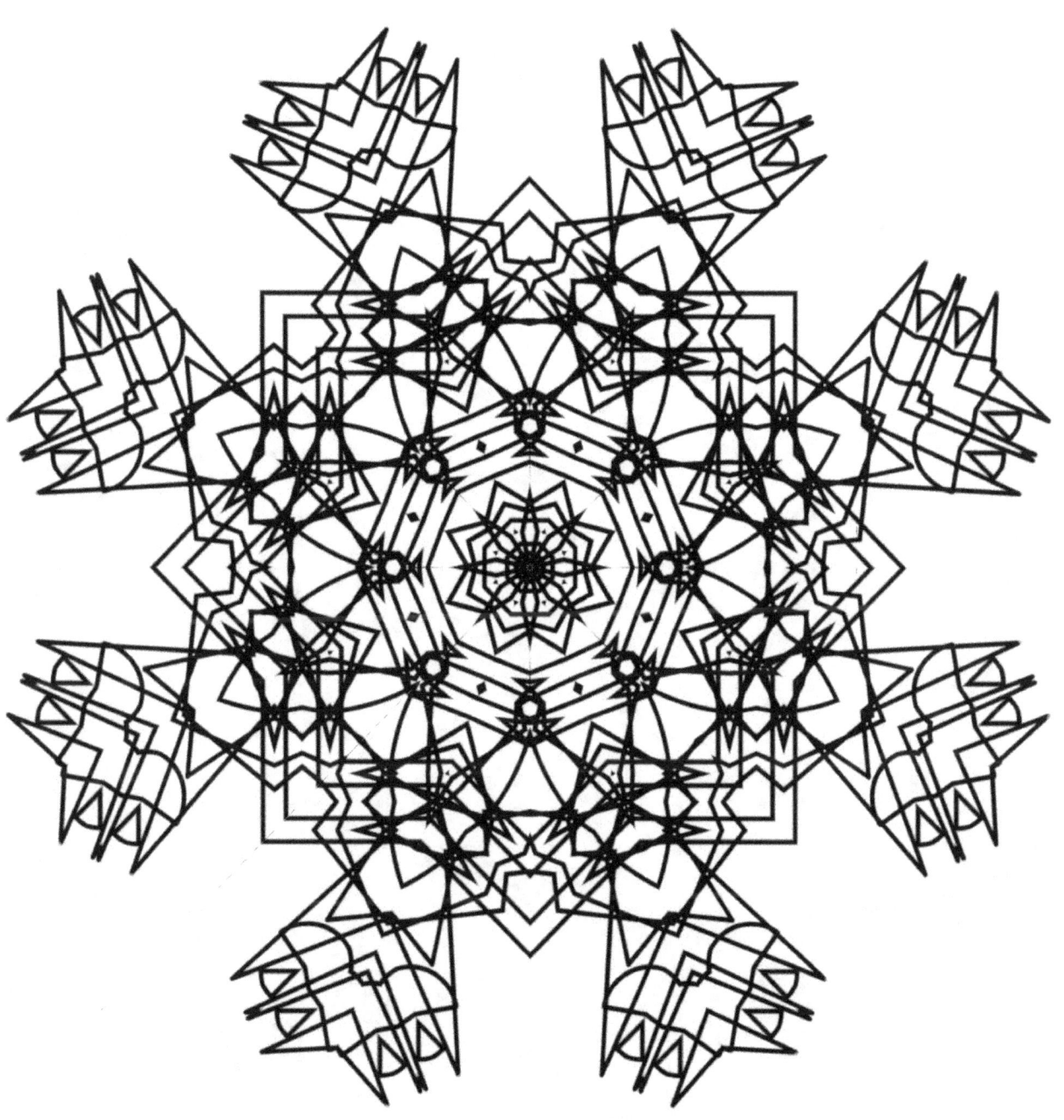

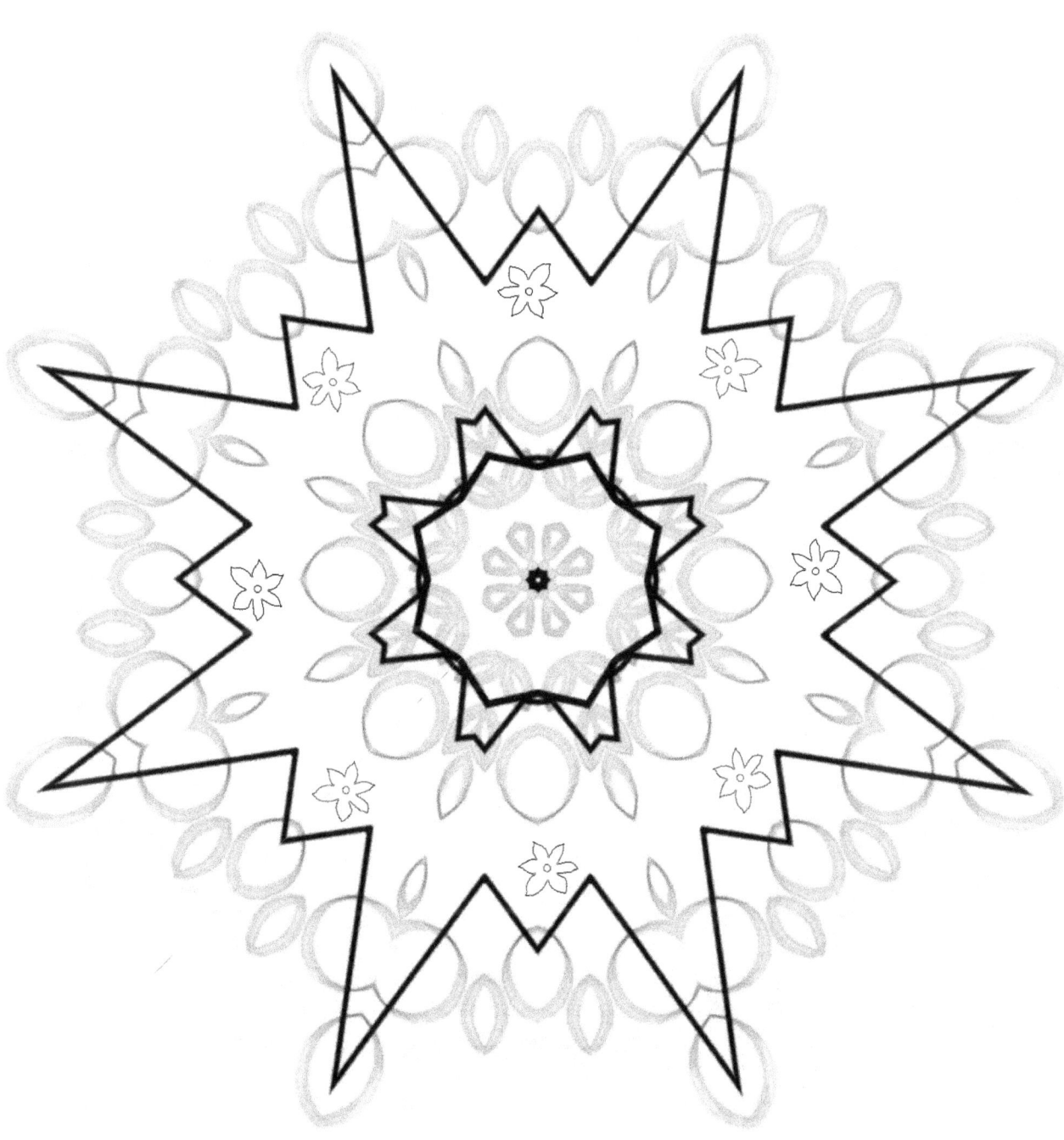

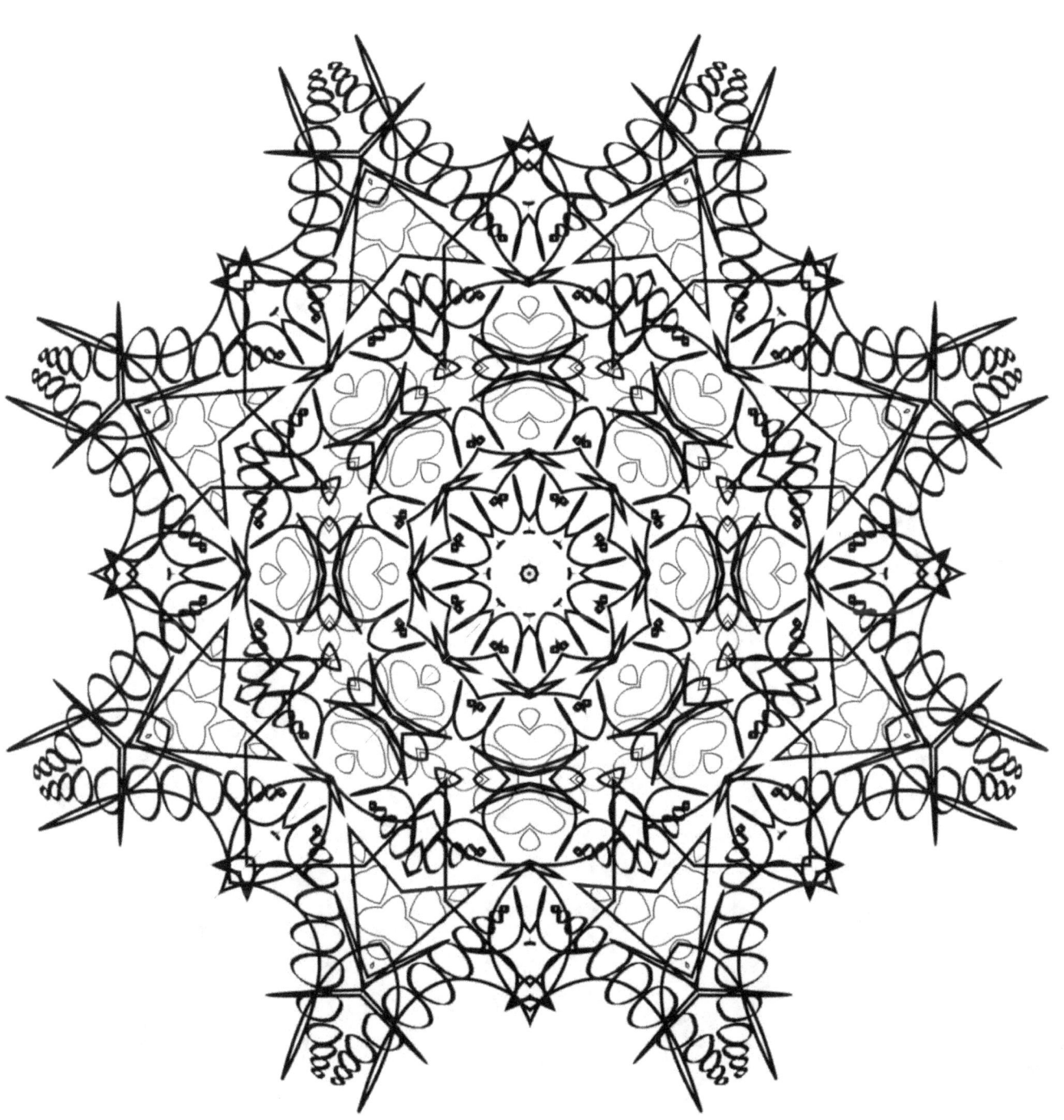

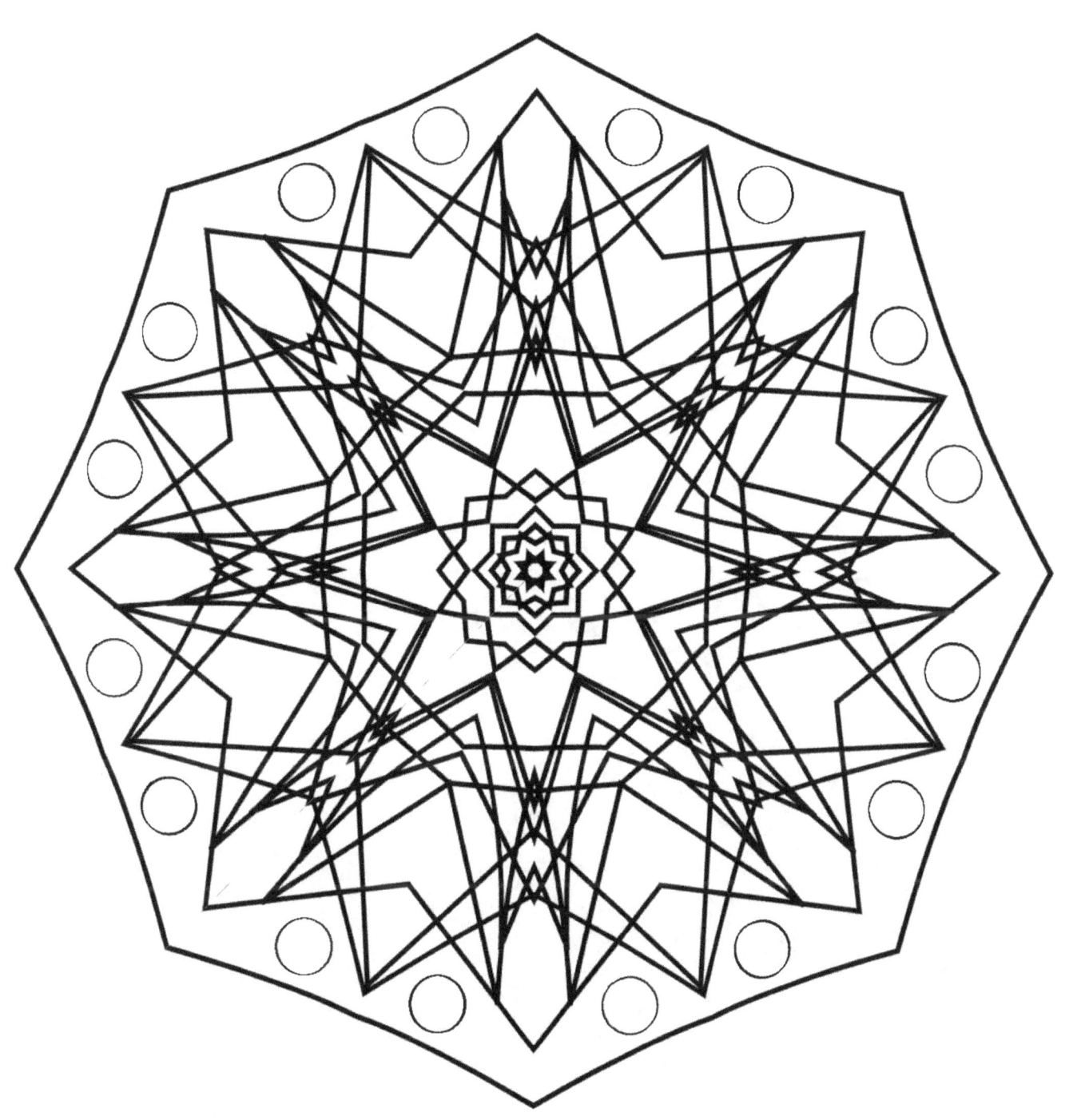

www.ingramcontent.com/pod-product-compliance
Lightning Source LLC
Chambersburg PA
CBHW081310170526
45166CB00011B/3475